All the best

Todd Rainey

Money
Talk

A Gay and Lesbian
Guide to Financial Success

About the Author

Todd Rainey is both a Chartered Life Underwriter (CLU) and a Chartered Financial Consultant (ChFC) who began his career in the financial services industry in 1986. He was in the top three percent of the advisors of one of the largest financial companies in the country, and a qualifying member of the Million Dollar Round Table (MDRT) which is comprised of the top five percent of the insurance industry professionals in the world.

Todd hosts the TV program *Money Talk* which is broadcast twice per month and seen in all of Los Angeles and vicinity. His charitable activities include serving as Treasurer of the Asian Pacific Gays and Friends, and he was President of the Valley Business Alliance, a business and charitable organization in the San Fernando Valley suburb of Los Angeles.

In business, Todd is the current (1999) President of the Brentwood Chapter of the Business Network International, an organization with 1,200 chapters in 20 countries around the globe, with members from all fields of business. In politics, Todd is the former President of the Log Cabin Republican Club in Ventura. This group fights homophobia in the Republican Party.

Todd's specialty is working with individuals, professionals and business owners to create a sound financial program which produces a desirable quality of life today and a future where financial concerns are eliminated. Todd can be reached by calling (818) 788-4719 or writing to him at Rainey, Kiley and Associates, 15456 Ventura Blvd. #202, Sherman Oaks, CA 91403.

Money
Talk

A Gay and Lesbian
Guide to Financial Success

by
Todd Rainey

GABRIEL PUBLICATIONS

ISBN #1-891689-75-4
LC # 99-65684
Cover design: Edwin Santiago
Typesetting: Synergistic Data Systems
sdsdesign@earthlink.net
Editor: Meridian Associates
MeridianOL@aol.com

Printed in United States of America

Dedication

In loving memory to Byron and Nellie Rainey, my grandparents, for their belief in me and for encouraging me to follow my heart's desires. I only wish they were here to see this book; they are both "expressed" within these pages-even if its between the lines. I couldn't have done it without you, Grandma and Grandpa. I love you.

Acknowledgments

I am deeply grateful to the following individuals for their heartfelt contributions to this book. Each brought their own expertise and insight either to the project itself, or my life as a whole.

- Rennie Gabriel, my publisher, for his editorial guidance and expertise throughout this project. Rennie is a fellow professional and an author in the field of financial advisement, and his knowledge and experience in the publishing business has been invaluable to me.

- Wendy Taylor, my copy editor and creative advisor for her professional overview, proofreading and editing of the material. She gave me gentle editorial suggestions, as well as what I could not provide for myself: faith and support for my writing.

- Edwin Santiago, for his friendship and support over these many years, and for his art and creativity in the layout and design for the cover of this book. He has captured the heart of my intention in his graphic design.

- Dr. Scott Lankford, for his kind assistance and endorsement of my book, and his fine work in writing the foreword.

- Anthony Nguyen, for his help in putting me in contact with Dr. Lankford and his constant words of encouragement throughout the writing of this book.

- My family, including: My grandparents Byron and Nellie Rainey, who both died within four months of each other, shortly before publication of this book, for their lifelong belief in me. My mother, Merleen Smith, for her love and reassurance to keep going —no matter what. To my father Robert Rainey for his love and support.

- Karen Hudson, for creating the basic manuscript from my resource materials. Without her start this would have been very difficult.

- Alec, my friend and partner. Thank you for your love and support.

- My clients and friends who said they would all "pick up a copy" of this book when it comes out . . . just because I wrote it, and because they care!

Table of Contents

Chapter Three

Chapter Four

Chapter Five

Chapter Seven

Foreword

In American education, it often seems like anything remotely important for the actual reality of living is left out entirely. Lawyers graduate from the best law schools in America without any training in how to actually handle themselves in a courtroom. Professors step into a classroom for the first time without any guidance about how to teach. We struggle through high school geometry and trig, but no one ever actually teaches how to balance a checkbook or understand the principal of compound interest. Similarly, high school textbooks treat gay/lesbian/bisexual people as if we didn't exist. It's all part of the same syndrome. In psych courses it's called Denial.

As an openly gay college professor in California, I've watched a whole generation of gay, lesbian, and bisexual students come out on campus, graduate from college, and take their place in the gay community. I've also worked to help create the nation's first domestic partners health benefits programs for professors, both at my own college and at my alma mater, Stanford University. All these lives, all these struggles, all these stories were about love and commitment, about self-respect, self-sacrifice, and pride in who we are and who we love. But they were also, in one way or another, stories about money, stories about having the financial resources to make our dreams come true.

That's what makes Todd Rainey's new book about successful financial management for the gay community so important. Rainey is right. Money Talks. It speaks the language of equality, power, and pride. This is especially true as we turn the corner to the twenty-first century, and a whole new chapter in the story of gay, lesbian, and bisexual identity as increasingly successful and powerful partners in mainstream America.

When I was growing up in the 1960's, money and sex were things most Americans were too embarrassed (or afraid) to talk about in public. It's no accident that one of the best-selling books of the era was titled *Everything You Ever Wanted To Know About Sex, But Were Afraid to Ask*. You bet we were afraid to ask (especially if we happened to be gay, lesbian, or bisexual). Straight or gay, we were taught to feel embarrassed, inadequate, and stupid for having any questions at all about the "facts of life." It didn't matter if the facts were physical or financial. You just weren't supposed to ask. You were just supposed to somehow "know," or maybe learn it all "on the street." When it came to sex and money, we were told, either you "had it" or you didn't. If you didn't —if you were different —then you sure better not be dumb enough to ask about it openly, because it must mean there was something secretly wrong with you. You must not be Normal. You must not be Average. You must not be In. You must not be Cool. You must be Queer.

No surprise, then, that the few paragraphs devoted to "homosexuality" in *Everything You Ever Wanted To Know About Sex* made us sound sick, sorry, and sad. It didn't matter that such stereotypes were obsolete already. The straight media said the Gay Rights Movement was part of the so-called Sexual Revolution, but they got it wrong, as usual. At its core, the gay rights movement was about money, political power and sheer survival—about the right of gay businesses and gay neighborhoods to even exist without being shut down by gay bashers, homophobic politicians, and out-of-control police.

In the decades since Stonewall, the power of the ballot box has been a major element in the struggle for basic dignity, equality, and civil rights. So have political campaign contributions from the gay community. It's no accident that Harvey Milk, the first openly gay elected official in America (and the gay community's first martyr) was a gay businessman and entrepreneur long before becoming a successful politician. In the political arena, the power of the Gay Dollar has been growing ever since. During the 1990's, the success (or failure) of presidential candidates was often determined in no small part by who would (or wouldn't) accept political campaign contributions from gay organizations within their own parties.

In art as in politics, the equation between money and sheer survival remains as strong as ever. The high profile battles in the arts in the 1990's were all about funding—who got it, who didn't (especially if those who got it were gay or lesbian). Even Ellen's notorious lesbian kiss on national TV came down to a matter of ratings and advertising dollars. In Tony Kushner's Tony-Award-winning play *Angels in America* (arguably the single most important theater event of the last quarter century), the vicious closet-case character Roy Cohn denies that he is "queer" precisely because he thinks gay people have no political or financial power. Since Cohn has plenty of money, and plenty of power, he tells himself, nobody can possibly call him queer. In a sick sort of way, Cohn (who died of AIDS) was right. When money talks, people listen.

In everyday life, most of us are far more worried about paying our rent than we are about which tuxedo we should wear to the next $1,000 per plate political fundraiser. But even in the workaday world, love and money get mixed together powerfully. It may be true, as the old song says, that "money can't buy love." But it can buy a bouquet of flowers for the one you love, or would like to.

For gay/lesbian/bisexual couples seeking to make their way together in the world, to buy a house together or maybe even to raise a family, money matters even more. Having the savings to make your dreams come true is just as important as having enough faith and patience to get through the next lover's quarrel. Love, faith, patience, and a healthy sense of humor to make it together in the long run—you will need them all, and more. The ability to manage money, to make sound financial decisions, is an indispensable element in any successful long-term relationship, straight or gay.

In America, honesty and integrity can be costly commodities. In my career as a college professor, I've watched literally dozens of gay completely on their own because their families disowned them. The good news is that such students often form their own "informal families" and financial support networks from groups of friends, both straight and gay. It's a sad reality that some still don't make it. The suicide rate for gay teens in America is still a national catastrophe. But the vast majority come out stronger and smarter—and more financially successful—precisely because they learned so early to take care of themselves and the people that they love. Often enough, they are the ones I see starting businesses and launching exciting new careers while their straight friends are still stuck in their low-paying, dead-end, dull McJobs. You don't have to tell students who just worked their way through college that 'Money talks.' They tell you.

In American media, money speaks to us primarily through advertising, and the images about ourselves it sells or shatters. In the bad old days, the mass-media stereotype was that gay people were powerless, poor, and invisible. The new media stereotype is that we're all cash-rich double-income Guppies (gay yuppies) with closets full of expensive designer clothes and wallets full of platinum charge cards. In the bad old days, ads for cigarettes or alcohol were funded by homophobic foundations which wanted to outlaw our existence. Now, the very same cigarette and alcohol companies sponsor high-profile gay-pride events around the country (killing us softly, some might say). When one mentally ill gay man goes crazy and murders Gianni Versace, straight America sees it all live on CNN, shakes their heads, and decides we must all be That Way. Some of us even buy into the same stereotypes ourselves. We run up huge credit card bills trying to look as rich and stylish as the media says we supposed to be, mortgaging our future to pay for a fantasy. But fantasy is fleeting, and minimum interest payments are forever. There's not much future in foreclosure.

There's a positive side to our new media image, fortunately. It's great to see more gay and lesbian characters on TV sit-coms, in films, and in shirtless designer jeans ads for clothes we can't afford. On the financial side, modern financial services like credit cards

On the financial side, modern financial services like credit cards and computers and bank ATM's really can help you manage your money more effectively. But, as a college professor, what I see all too often are high-pressure sales people coming up on campus, offering to help students take on disastrous debts with no down-payment, high-interest scams. Government-sponsored student loans are now easier to get than ever. For students seeking a college degree that can be good news. Yet, all too often those students emerge from college loaded down with enough debt to qualify as a third-world country. For those in similar financial trouble, *Money Talk* may be the best investment you ever made in your own education.

In many ways, the gay, lesbian, and bisexual students I see coming through college today have more assets than they realize. They have courage. They have love. They have a healthy sense of humor about themselves, and a wild sixth-sense for the ironies and hypocrisies of the world around them. They have creativity. They have commitment. They have grace. They have youth. They have vision. They have cell phones, pagers, and multiple Internet email addresses. Some of them even have tattoos, fierce haircuts, and multiple body piercings. What they don't have, despite all the media stereotypes to the contrary, is much money, or much training in how to handle it.

There is no doubt that today's college and high school students are coming out of the closet earlier than any generation in American history. Many of the students I meet through our Gay/Straight Student Alliance at Foothill College came out years before coming to college. Others (like me) waited until after college before taking those first frightened steps toward greater honesty, integrity, and freedom. Many are still waiting for the "right time" to come out. But waiting to come out until after college doesn't necessarily make things any easier either. After graduation, many gay students move in together, start relationships that might last a month and might last a lifetime, moving to big, expensive urban areas where the gay community is well-established. For recent graduates like these, I'm convinced Todd Rainey's *Money Talk* can make a major positive difference in the overall quality and character of their lives. In my Gay Utopian University (GUU) , it would be part of a required course called Life 101. As graduates of GUU, the basic life lessons *Money Talk* teaches can spell the difference between making it in the world on your own terms and being forced back into the closet by financial fears. Every time you rent an apartment, every time you fill out a job application, every time you introduce yourself to a new client or supervisor, you have to decide, one more time, whether to come out or hide from who you are. It's a whole lot easier to handle homophobia if you feel financially stable and emotionally secure.

Historically, one of the main reasons the gay community has survived and thrived is that we knew how to take care of ourselves, how to take care of our own. In the golden age of gay rights, it meant finding the finances to renovate previously run-down neighborhoods such as San Francisco's Castro district or New York's Soho. It also meant finding the money to open gay-friendly businesses, often in the same neighborhoods, where we didn't have to be afraid anymore, where we didn't have to hide. Later, in the era of AIDS, it meant raising money for research, education, outreach and support programs. Increasingly, it has meant raising money to support gay-rights political platforms, legislation, and candidates across the nation. On the job, it has meant insisting on equal pay for equal work, including equal health benefits for our partners and our families.

In America at the beginning of the twenty-first century, the idea that a black or Jewish family is not entitled to the same health benefits as other employees would be considered racist and absurd. Yet the idea that gay employees and their families are not entitled to the same benefits, solely because of the gender of the people they happen to love, is still enshrined in laws and employment contracts all across the country. On my own campus, the fact that we were fighting for financial equality, not just social "tolerance," helped many of my older colleagues find the strength to stand up for themselves for the first time in their long and distinguished professional careers. Professors who had lived for decades in monogamous, committed, loving relationships finally found the courage to ask their colleagues to recognize, to honor, and to support the sanctity of their relationships in real terms. Money talks. Sometimes it even helps you hear your own conscience more clearly.

For people my age and older, Todd Rainey's book can be an invaluable asset. Being out on our own for a longer period of time hasn't always left us better prepared to deal with financial reality. Too often, we've postponed sober-sounding tasks like financial planning until after the party's over. Since the party is never over (unless you want it to be), solid financial planning gets postponed indefinitely. We're not alone. Statistically, researchers confirm that Americans are spending more, and saving less, than at any time in our history. Like coming out, it's easy to postpone financial planning forever. "Tomorrow," we tell ourselves. "When the time is right," we say. But tomorrow never comes. Like coming out, solid financial planning gives us the power and perspective and even the pride in ourselves to make the magic happen now, not tomorrow, or someday, or never. It's about learning to imagine our own future, instead of letting other people imagine it for us. It's about learning to take control of our own personal life, our own financial destiny.

If you focus on what you can't do in the short-term rather than what you can do in the long run, being "financially responsible" sounds like about as much fun as oral surgery. Todd Rainey's *Money Talk* makes the whole process seem more like sitting down with a close friend, someone you trust, and talking about how to make your dreams come true.

Think of it this way (if you dare): Back in the days of American slavery, the first rule for slave owners was simple: Never teach a slave to read. Ignorance is slavery. Knowledge is power. In the world of money and personal financial planning, it works pretty much the same way. *Money Talk* is about freedom. It's also about making some choices, here and now. Treating gay people as if they never existed means we have no rights. It also means we have no money. No dignity. No history. No voice. No clout. No future.

Learning to talk the language of money won't make you materialistic. But it might make you angry. Think of how many gay, lesbian, and bisexual people have been fired from their jobs, or thrown out of their apartments, or kicked out of their families, all because they chose to remain true to themselves and the ones they love. Think of the money raised to fight AIDS, to support gay-friendly candidates and causes, to build community centers and fund gay pride festivals. The Big Lie the straight world tells about gay people is that we are defined by our sexuality, hence the clinical term "homosexuality," which sounds more like a disease than a way of life, a way of being, a kind of love. The real secret, the one they don't want anyone to know, because it would change everything, is as simple as it is powerful. Being gay is all about love. About who you choose to spend your life with, and why.

Believe it. Invest in your dreams. Invest in your community. Invest in yourself, in the people you love, and in the causes you care for. Turn the page. Open a new chapter, right here, right now.

—Scott Lankford, Ph.D.
Professor of English
Foothill College
Los Altos Hills, California

Chapter One

We Know That
We Are Different

I've got all the money I'll ever need
if I die by four o'clock.
                                    —Henny Youngman

Since you are reading this book, chances are that you are gay or lesbian, or at least have an interest in gay and lesbian finances. What you probably haven't considered is that there are many differences in how we spend and save our money.

This book is not intended to tell you what to do with your financial future. Rather, the goal is to give you an education so that you can make decisions that will give you the prosperous future that you want and deserve.

The following information is from a recent government census and insurance company mortality data. Studies say that for every 100 people that start their careers at the age of 22, the following situation exists at age 65:

- 20 people are dead, they never made it to age 65. About 1 in 5 people don't even live through the 40 years of work to retire at age 65. If you think for a moment, there are probably several people you know of personally who've died before age 65. It's not just AIDS, but heart disease, cancer, smoking related deaths, auto accidents and more.

• 19 people will have an income of $7,500 or less, *per year!* The poverty level for 1990 was only $6,300 per year, so this would be about $100 per month more than the poverty level.

• 44 people out of one hundred will have income between $7,500 and $30,000 per year. The *median* is the halfway point. The median income is $14,500 per year, or roughly $1,208 per month. Can you picture yourself today living for the next 25 years, or longer, on $1,200 per month? And this includes Social Security.

• 17 people would have an annual income in excess of $30,000 per year, or $2,500 per month. This is fewer than one out of five. And, only five people out of these 17 would have an annual income over $40,000. These are the five that we would consider financially successful at age 65. My goal is to give you the tools so you will be one of the five who are considered "financially successful."

While the figures above may be based on incomes in the 1990's, don't dwell on the specific income figures. Inflation will have made these income figures higher, the percentage of the population near the poverty level will still be around 19%. The percentage of people who struggle with an inadequate income will still be around 44%. These percentages have remained virtually unchanged since 1970 when they were compiled by the Department of Health, Education and Welfare.

Most of us, being gay or lesbian, do not have dependent spouses to support and children to raise. Therefore, we don't have expensive weddings or ruinous divorces to worry about. This gives us the ability to create more disposable income. Disposable income is money you have left after paying for all the necessary things in life such as food, clothing and shelter. What's left is so-called disposable income. This is the money with which you make choices, like buying a car, going on vacation, getting an entertainment center or pursuing your hobby. Anyway, that's what is supposed to happen.

In addition to the choices we have to spend this money, we can choose to save or invest it. Unfortunately, a recent study by the Department of Health & Human Services indicated 85% of the population tends to live from paycheck to paycheck. As I've said, only 5% of us retire comfortably.

The key is to use this disposable income in a way that can convert today's dollars into tomorrow's wealth. Many times I have said, "The only person who you can count on to take care of the old person you will one day become is the younger person that you are today."

Gays and lesbians often make successful entrepreneurs simply because many of us are loners, not expecting much support, being quick on our feet, adapting to whatever we encounter, and monitoring our environment carefully. This allows a great opportunity which can be used to our advantage. The opportunity is to have the freedom to be entrepreneurial and risk-takers without the added fear of a family to depend on us.

Financial success is defined by whom you ask. We all must define this for ourselves. We have been given a great opportunity to achieve and appreciate a high quality of life, for ourselves and the community at large. Are you ready to pursue the goal of gay financial freedom?

Fundamental Development Differences

Teens

Straight teens often have a chance to work out their identities with family and peer support. There are numerous role models and societal models with which they can identify and build their lives around.

Gay teens live in a world of isolation, AIDS publicity, backlash, and a community of elders decimated by the AIDS epidemic. In addition, there are very few role models and virtually no societal models with which a gay teen can identify. The number of gay teens committing suicide soars to three times that of their straight counterparts. As a result, gay teens are about survival. Thus, as a result of our environment, many of us become the loners, entrepreneurs, business owners, and so on that help to create one of the most financially successful segments in the American society.

Twenties

The straight 20's are motivated by the possibility of marriage and children. Again, the society shapes the way we think about ourselves and our roles in society, and there are numerous visions with which to identify.

Many twenty-something gays, having survived the isolation of youth, emerge into the heaven of freedom. It is usually in the early 20's that we begin to identify with our sexuality and begin to date. At this age, we are the prizes of our community. Gays in their early 20's are often concerned with their physical body and appearance. We are quite sexual, and as a result, are sought after by young and old alike. Gays are usually unburdened with the notion of a family, thus are free to pursue their own endeavors. Choices we make at this stage of life can help to set us up for a great success later in life.

Thirties

Most straights marry and begin planning for a family. Their lives are about building and providing for their families.

Gays in their 30's often drift financially. Since the pressures surrounding building a family do not exist, we often spend time being obsessed with our looks and health, and worry about little else. Under the best circumstances, gays use the 30's to build careers, investments, relationships, and real estate. Surprisingly, a little attention to details at this stage of life will reward you substantially in a relatively few years.

Forties

The straight forties begins the emptying of the nest. Children head off to college and begin their own lives and careers. Many straight people are now free to begin their planning for retirement.

The gay 40's is a time for taking stock of the advantages we gained in our 30's and the results of our actions. It's time for a reality check. This is when we may realize we missed out on all espousal benefits. While we escape the tax code's marriage penalty, many financial supports for relationships are missing. Under current tax law, married couples filing jointly actually pay a larger tax rate than single individuals. Of course, tax laws are never constant as they can and do change. There are other benefits to being married, such as employer benefits, unlimited gifts between spouses and dual income, which are not usually offered to gays.

Fifties

For the straight world, the 50's see wives passing through menopause, moving toward independence while men may go through a male menopause or mid-life crisis themselves. This can leave them stronger and re-focused, or searching for meaning in their lives. This is also the time when men reach the peak of their income. At this time, income seems to level off and there is more to save and invest for retirement because the children are usually building their own lives.

For gays, this is when gay discrimination occurs, especially in our own community. Gay men in their fifties tend to be invisible to the community as a whole. They no longer blend into the larger gay community. Many have a small circle of friends or "extended families" with which they surround themselves. Due to the toll of AIDS, a great number of gay men in their 50's have vanished. If they are alive and single, they tend to remove themselves from the "gay environment," move to the suburbs and blend into the larger community as a whole.

5

Sixties and Seventies

This can be a time of blossoming and enjoying the grandchildren for straight people.

Gays have extended friendship circles and families of choice to offset a lack of children or grandchildren. Hopefully for gays, they have sufficient investment income to offset a lack of espousal pensions, and this book is designed to move you beyond hope and into financial independence as a reality. Many gays have created a legacy which will tie them to future generations through the businesses they have built. Restaurants, hair salons, travel and tourist services, as well any of the same types of businesses created by the straight people, will continue on after retirement or death. This concept is explained further in the book Gay Money *by Per Larson.*

In my work throughout the community, I have known many gay couples that have been together for 20 to 30 years, and longer. In many cases, these people have no contact at all with their birth relatives. I find that during the holidays and special occasions these couples have large gatherings of friends (family) who fill that role left vacant by the lack of children and other relatives.

Now that we are aware of our financial differences, let's see how we can restructure ourselves to take advantage of our differences.

Chapter Two

Financial Planning
— It's a Process

You can't hope to be lucky.
You have to prepare to be lucky.

—Timothy Down

I wish that I could tell you that the financial planning process is easy and that all of you will one day be wealthy. What I can tell you is that the "process" is simple. While the process is simple, having the discipline and foresight to *keep on track and follow the plan* is never easy. However, if you use the concepts of this book and stay focused on your goals, financial freedom can be yours.

The key word here is *process*. Below, I have listed the six steps involved in the financial planning process. Nonetheless, when you deal with money and investing, your actual results can never be guaranteed. One thing is for sure, you are always better off if you plan and prepare rather than do nothing at all. And since you are in fact reading this book, I assume you are serious about planning your financial future.

Financial Planning is a Six-Step Process:

1. Establishing financial goals—know where you are going.

2. Gathering data—know where you are now.

3. Processing and analyzing data—what are you missing?

4. Developing a financial plan—how do you get from here to there?

5. Implementing the plan—getting started.

6. Monitoring the plan—keeping your eye on the ball.

Establishing Your Financial Goals

These goals depend a lot on your range of desire. You may simply want to save for an expensive purchase, or plan for a longer range goal such as retirement. If you plan and invest well and build a substantial level of assets, as I hope you will, you may want to plan for an orderly distribution of your estate at the time of your death. The main thing is you need to have a vision of where you want to be, or, chances are, you will not get there! If you don't know where you want to be, or what you want to have, speak to others to find out what their plans are. Some things may fit, and others will not, but then you have some ideas from which to choose.

Gathering Data

Simply put, you need to know what is coming in, what is going out, and more importantly, what you are keeping. As my wise grandfather always told me, "It's not what you make that's important, it's what you keep." You'll also need to gather copies of important documents such as: Tax returns, life insurance policies, auto and homeowner policies, pension plans, IRA's, wills and trusts you've executed, as well as any other important documents.

Processing and Analyzing Data

After you have gathered this data you can determine if anything is missing in order for you to reach your goals. You will take a close look at what you have done, saved and invested so far, and where that can take you down the road. The second step is to look at what is necessary to reach your financial goal. If the resulting difference is a negative, it's called a *shortfall*. From here you can determine what is necessary to adjust in order to reach your ultimate goals.

Developing a Financial Plan

If you have completed the first three steps, and have accurately calculated your shortfall, then you are in a position to reach those goals. With proper asset class selections and investment choices, which we will discuss in chapter four, you will be well on your way to achieving your financial objectives.

Implementing the Plan

This is where the rubber meets the road. You must keep your focus on your goals and do what it takes. More wise words from my grandfather, "Do something, even if it's wrong . . . do something!" Not to take anything from my grandfather, but I think it is much better to do the right thing rather than the wrong. But seriously, this is where people either start down the way to a better financial future, or continue down the road more traveled but far less fulfilling.

Monitoring Your Plan

Life changes. You need to make the appropriate changes to your plan to meet your changing life and goals. Life is not stagnate; as your life changes, so will your goals. When you are in your early 30's you may have a goal of purchasing a home or starting a business. In your 40's your goals may have changed to purchasing some rental property. And, in your fifties, perhaps retirement is on the forefront of your mind. As your goals change, you need to make adjustments.

Balance Sheet — Knowing Your Net Worth

Your assets are anything you own, and your liabilities are everything that you owe. Below we have listed a partial list of assets and liabilities that you will commonly find in most balance sheets.

Assets

✓ All the cash that you have in your possession right now

✓ All monies in your checking accounts

✓ All monies in your saving accounts

✓ Money Market accounts

✓ Certificates of Deposit (*CD's include accrued interest; exclude future interest and possible penalties for early withdrawal*)

✓ Cash value of life insurance policies

Invested Assets

✓ U.S. government bonds/foreign government bonds

✓ Corporate bonds

✓ Corporate stocks

✓ Mutual funds

✓ Investment real estate

✓ Partnership interests

✓ Limited liability company interest

✓ Sole proprietorship interests

✓ Individual retirement accounts (IRA)

✓ Vested portion of pension plans

✓ Any other investments

Use Assets (Real Property)

✓ Residence

✓ Vacation home

✓ Vehicles

✓ Personal property

✓ Artwork

✓ Collectibles

Liabilities

✓ Credit card balances

✓ Vehicle loans

✓ Student loans

✓ Bank loans

✓ Mortgages

✓ Other loans

✓ Any back taxes owed

A *balance sheet* represents the major step in creating financial freedom; finding out where you are now. It is a list of everything you own and everything you owe. It's like a snapshot of your overall financial picture, and only reflects the moment in time when you fill it in. The next moment your cash could be higher or lower. The balance sheet will show if you are in a positive or negative financial position. You may see how some items can produce income for you when you choose to stop working for a living, and others will not. As an example, equity in a home produces no income to buy groceries.

The value in seeing this snapshot is the opportunity to create a *'before and after'* financial picture. Whether it is three months, six months, or one year from now, take this picture again. This is how you will measure your progress. You will see if you have more cash in the bank, newer cars, more investments, or less debt each time you take a new picture. The objective is to create a large, investable, *Net Worth.* This is the amount you would have left over if you sold everything you owned to pay off everything you owed. Again, *Assets* are everything you own. *Liabilities* are everything you owe. If you subtract what you owe from what you own, it's called Net Worth. You won't be selling everything off, but it's the measurement to show you how close you're getting to financial freedom.

The following is a form for your personal use. To compute your net worth, place your assets in the left column and your liabilities in the right column.

The Balance Sheet

Assets		Liabilities	
Home (FMV)*	$_____	Home Mortgage(s)	$_____
Other Real Estate	_____	*(Outstanding Balance)*	
Other Real Estate	_____	Other R.E. loans	_____
Personal property	_____		_____
Vested retirement	_____		
IRA's	_____	Other: Auto, boat, credit cards,	
Listed Securities	_____	family loans, pool loan, notes,	
Stock options	_____	past income taxes, etc.	
Life Ins. (Cash value)	_____		
Business interest:		Item: _____	$_____
Accounts receivable	_____		_____ _____
Inventory / equip.	_____		_____ _____
Cash / retained earn.	_____		_____ _____
Goodwill	_____		
Personal Savings	_____		
Money Market acct	_____	TOTAL LIABILITIES	$_____
Certificates of Deposit	_____		
Checking account	_____		
Autos _____	_____		
	_____		
Other _____	_____		
(Art, jewelry, antiques)			
TOTAL ASSETS	$_____	NET WORTH	$_____
F.M.V. = Fair Market Value		*(Subtract Liabilities from Assets)*	

If your input information is accurate, your bottom line will also be accurate with the asset amount being equal to the total of the net worth and liability amounts. Again, keep in mind your net-worth is a moving target and is only a snapshot of one moment in time. There's no secret to knowing your net worth. If you have a partner and you maintain separate finances, an individual balance sheet for each of you may be more appropriate. If not, do a joint balance sheet. If you have difficulty in dealing with joint finances, we will discuss "domestic partnership agreements" later in this book.

Using Your Balance Sheet

Consider the following uses of the balance sheet as a tool to help you in your financial planning:

1. *Insurance planning tool.* Your balance sheet can be an important source of information for risk management and insurance planning. The balance sheet also can provide a few clues about your need for life insurance. If your balance sheet includes liabilities that would be a burden on a loved one in the event of your premature death, you'll want to be certain your life insurance coverage is sufficient to satisfy the liabilities—for example, if you have a mortgage on your home and would like to provide your partner with a enough insurance to eliminate that debt and provide a free and clear home instead of a large liability. A life insurance policy would be appropriate for this purpose.

2. *Investment planning tool.* A quick review of the relative values of your invested assets can give a rough idea of whether your portfolio is properly allocated among the various types of investments. Studies have shown that this area is the most critical in determining your

portfolio's overall rate of return. It has been shown that proper asset class selection contributes up to 91.5% of a portfolio's return. (Investing at the right time provides a mere 8.5% o the return.)

3. *Retirement planning tool.* An important part of the retirement planning process requires identifying how much you should save and invest to meet your retirement income needs. To do this, you need to understand first how much you currently have available to apply toward your goal. Remember, what you "spend" now will never return; what you save and invest now will be with you for life.

4. *Estate planning tool.* In order to decide how you want your assets disposed of when you die, you need to identify what those assets are.

5. *Measuring progress toward goals.* Many of your financial goals will not be accomplished immediately. Something such as saving for retirement will require long-term savings and investing strategies. Preparing annual balance sheets and comparing each year's figures with those from the prior year can help you measure your progress toward your goals. This will also help you see if you are on track, or if you may need to adjust your plan accordingly.

The Emergency Fund

One other important use of the balance sheet that deserves special consideration is for identifying an *emergency fund.* The purpose of the emergency fund is to provide a ready source of cash in the event of a financial emergency, thereby avoiding the need to liquidate assets, borrow at unreasonable interest rates, or endure other financial hardship.

Most financial planners recommend that an emergency fund contain sufficient resources to fund at least three months, and potentially up to six months, of your fixed and variable expenses.

While the evidence is anecdotal, many financial planners who serve the lesbian and gay community report that, as a group, we're not very good about saving for our emergency funds. Call it a "lifestyle thing" if you want, but it seems as though many of us don't have enough savings to fund our expenses for six weeks, let alone six months. A friend of mine once told me something that reminds me of the Henny Youngman quote. He said, "If I quit work today, I could live quite comfortably on my savings until next Thursday."

Building a Budget

A budget usually projects forward over a one year period, whereas a cash flow statement looks back over one year. The budget is important to establish your goals, and to have a plan to reach your goals. The cash-flow statement looks back at where you actually spent your money. This is helpful to illustrate where you can adjust, cut back, or eliminate unnecessary expenses in favor of more productive ones.

Inflows

Wages and salaries—This is earned income from an employer. Usually you will get a W2 on an annual basis.

Interest—From savings account, money market account, dividend income, etc. You will see this on a form 1099.

Other income—Rents, royalties, trust and retirement plan distributions, or self-employment income.

Outflows

Savings and investments—(Always place at the top of your list.) This is listed as an outflow from your income since you are "spending" this money on your savings & investments. This should be at least 10% of your annual income. As you get older, and as your income increases, the percentage of income you save and/or invest should increase as well.

Housing expenses—Mortgage, rent, utilities, repairs insurance.

Vehicle expense—Loan payment, lease, insurance, gasoline repairs, tires, planned maintenance such as tires and brakes, auto insurance.

Other debts—Credit card payments (keep to a minimum), loan payments to banks or individuals, debt service, etc.

Insurance premiums—Life, health, disability income, long-term care, liability and renters or homeowners insurance.

Variable Outflows

These are the expenses which may come in each month, or at various times during the year, and will vary in amount. By looking at how much they are on an annual basis you can set aside the money to cover them by saving up for it on a monthly basis. As an example, if you only purchased clothing once per year and spent $1,200, you could set aside $100 per month toward that eventual expense.

Taxes—Income, property, vehicle.
Food
Transportation—Auto, air, train.
Clothing
Entertainment/vacations
Health care
Utilities/household expenses
Contribution—Charitable gifts, family gifts.
Other expenses

Managing Consumer Debt

*Credit (kred'it) – The process of purchasing
something you don't need, at a price you can't afford,
with money you don't have.*

—Todd Rainey

If you have a credit card, you should never carry a balance. If you only made the minimum payment, it would take you twenty years to pay them off. This is good for the credit card company and bad for you. By living within your budget and avoiding spending money you don't have, you will make *yourself* rich, rather than the credit card company. Try to eliminate all current balances. If you have trouble controlling your spending, cut up your credit cards and throw them away. If you can manage self control, credit cards are a helpful tool. Many credit cards have an 18–22% interest rate; that's a lot of interest which could be used for investments instead. See how much you can free up to pay down the balances.

Consider the following to handle credit card debt (in order of severity):

1. Switch your balances to lower interest cards. Many credit card companies offer low interest rates from three months to one year on balance transfers from another card.

2. Read one or both of the following books: *Wealth On Any Income* by Rennie Gabriel, and/or *How To Get Out of Debt* by Jerrold Mundis.

3. Consider refinancing your mortgage, but only if you lower your monthly payment sufficiently. If you do refinance your home and use cash from your equity to pay off credit card debt, <u>DO NOT</u> make the mistake of running up the balances on your credit cards again or you will be in a worse position.

4. Consider consolidating your debt with a home equity loan. This is the same situation as refinancing your mortgage. It could be a good idea if you really do pay off the debt you have, but you do have to weigh the cost involved.

5. Get a second job.

6. Contact the credit card companies to arrange the possibility of working out an extended repayment schedule. You need to be aware that doing so will cause you to pay significantly more interest, due to having a larger balance over an extended time period. Also, this could negatively impact your credit rating.

7. Consider borrowing against other assets to pay off the cards. Here again pay attention to the costs involved and be careful not to "rob Peter to pay Paul."

8. Contact your lender to see if your loans can be recalculated to reduce the payments. This as well will increase your overall interest costs, and could negatively impact your credit.

9. Sell assets. There is usually a significant loss when you liquidate assets, unless it is real estate. I would consider this only in severe situations.

10. Consult an attorney to consider filing for bankruptcy. Bankruptcy should be considered only in the most severe situations. You will eliminate much of your debt and free up your cash flow, however, the ramifications of this action will follow you forever.

There are down-sides to some of these options. If your situation is serious, you should contact a credit counseling agency.

Strategies

1. It is important to set up an emergency fund to cover three to six months worth of fixed and variable outflows. This fund is your protection. Always pay it first. You should get in the habit of saving 10% of your income right off the top of each paycheck for this purpose.

2. After you have funded your emergency fund, then you can redirect that money into more long-term savings and investments. Your ability to do this will determine your success in the future.

3. Many gays are not married, and do not have the benefit (right) of survivorship benefits from pension plans or social security. Therefore, many of us may need to save even more for retirement than straight people do. Retirement planning is a cornerstone in a good financial plan. This is one area that will affect you for the rest of your life. Unlike many other goals which you can postpone or delay, once you have retired it's too late for retirement planning. Plan early and plan often, or the part-time job at McDonald's could become your retirement plan.

Chapter Three

Risk Management

Shallow men believe in luck;
wise and strong men in cause and effect.
—Ralph Waldo Emerson

A fundamental goal of financial planning is to reduce the risks. Without proper risk management, one catastrophic loss could wipe out an entire lifetime of savings.

An important rule for managing risk is through the use of insurance; this is known as *large loss principle*. This principle insures against events that are infrequent or unlikely, but with potentially high loss, such as a fire or death. You insure against these events because, unlike small losses which can happen more frequently but are easily paid for out of cash flow, large losses seldom happen—but when they do, the results are devastating.

Under this same principle, it would be more important for a single person with no dependents to protect his or her income while still alive, rather than insuring themselves against premature death. Therefore, disability insurance for gays could be considered be more important than life insurance.

Methods

Experts talk about risk in terms of how catastrophic the potential losses are, and how likely it is or how often the risk may become a reality.

There are four methods for handling risk:

1. *Risk avoidance.* The person does not engage in the activity producing the risk. For example, if the risk is dying in a plane crash, the risk avoidance would be not to fly.

2. *Risk retention.* The individual exposed to the risk assumes personal financial responsibility for its consequences. A good example would be to self insure all or a portion of the risk from your own cash-flow. A good example of this is the deductible imposed by a health insurance policy.

3. *Risk transfer.* The risk of loss is assumed by another entity. A good example is buying insurance to protect against the risk of a fire destroying your house.

4. *Risk reduction.* An example here would be to buy smoke detectors or sprinklers for your house to reduce the amount of damage from fire.

Life Insurance

Choosing an Insurer

Many gays and lesbians look at life insurance as unnecessary. I believe this to be a shortsighted view. There are many advantages to owning the proper insurance policy, some of which include: cash value accumulations, low interest or interest free loans, tax-deferred growth and the "living needs" rider. This permits a payment of up to 92% of the death benefit, tax free, upon diagnosis of a terminal illness. This could be a saving grace for many in the gay community.

Purchasing insurance coverage is a well-known risk management technique. It's important you purchase your coverage from a solid insurer. You should only buy a policy from companies that have the highest rating from several rating agencies.

Consider the company's size and experience. Large insurers that have been in business for many years tend to offer a higher level of assurance than newer firms. Cost should be a consideration, but should seldom be the deciding factor. Finally, look at the insurance company's financial performance. Ask your financial planner, broker, and/or agent for help in analyzing the figures.

Insurance companies tend not to give our community the consideration it deserves. The obvious solution is to work with an insurer from the community, if possible. You need an insurer who will be your advocate, and not someone with biases. Referrals from friends or colleagues are often a good way to choose a quality advisor.

Common Uses of Life Insurance

Maintaining a standard of living – In case of your death, your dependents can maintain their standard of living. In addition to spouses, children, and significant others, it contemplates parents, other family members, or anyone else who relies on you for economic support. You could even name a favorite charity.

Paying estate taxes – Individuals with a net worth in excess of $650,000 can expect to owe federal estate taxes when they die. They can use life insurance and end up paying pennies on the dollar for those taxes. This allows your heirs the option of selling assets to pay the estate taxes, or retaining them and using insurance to pay Uncle Sam.

Making charitable contributions – Depending on your circumstances, insuring your life and naming a charity as the beneficiary on the policy could create significant extra income for the organization and current tax deductions for you.

Protecting business interests – If a partner dies prematurely, the insurance proceeds can be used to buy out the partner's interest, providing cash for the partner's survivors and continuity of the business. Life insurance can also protect the business in the event of the death of a key employee, or assure an orderly transfer from parents to children.

Repaying debt – Life insurance can repay debts such as mortgage, credit cards, loans, etc. in the event of early death.

Final expense – Funeral arrangements are seldom cheap, but people of limited means can purchase enough life insurance coverage for a decent burial. With people on the other financial spectrum, life insurance can provide an immediate short-term cash flow, when an estate's assets are not liquid. Something seldom related to final expenses are medical costs. Even if you have medical insurance, there are often significant expenses that need to be paid and are not covered by medical insurance.

Tax-advantaged investing – Various types of insurance products build up value over time by allowing investments in mutual funds. Similar to building equity in your home, it grows on a tax-deferred basis. Over time, this can be a significant asset.

Forced savings – If you have trouble saving, several products provide a mechanism that "forces" you to save. Countless times over my 13 year career I have seen the cash value inside an insurance policy make a significant difference to a family during a difficult time.

Employee benefits – Group term life insurance is a fringe benefit provided by many employers. This can vary from the basic $10,000 to a multiple of your income. If it's free, take all you can get. If you have to pay, check the costs.

Non-qualified deferred compensation – This is a specialized form of life insurance and is used as a fringe benefit for key executives. It can provide current tax advantages, plus a larger retirement income, disability benefits and survivorship benefits.

Determining Insurance Needs

"How much life insurance, do I really need?" This depends on what your objective are. Traditionally, life insurance replaces income lost through premature death. Insurance professionals can give you specifics for your situation. Depending on your age, it usually takes between five and seven times your annual salary to generate a cash stream sufficient to replace your lost income.

Types of Life Insurance

The two basic types of life insurance are *term* insurance and *cash value,* or *permanent* insurance.

Term Insurance

Term insurance contracts provide life insurance protection for a *level premium* for a specific period of time. This could be for 1, 5, 10, 15, 20 or 30 years. You can buy an *annual renewable* policy which allows you to renew at the end of each year and, because you are one year older, the premium increases at each renewal term. If you die during the period of coverage, your beneficiaries collect your death benefit. If you're alive at the end, you get nothing. This insurance is less expensive over a short period of time, but the longer you pay the premium, the more expensive the policy becomes.

Term insurance provides death protection and nothing else, so the benefits are at a lower initial cost for the highest benefit. The disadvantage is the cost increases dramatically at older ages, it usually becomes unaffordable and ends up being canceled prior to death. Only about 3% of all term policies ever result in a claim. In the long run, *level premium term* usually is cheaper and generally is a better insurance buy. If your needs are short-term, *annual renewable* may make more sense. Just be sure your policy contains a renewal clause. Otherwise, your insurer may have the option not to renew your insurance, may require new medical underwriting or establish new higher rates.

Cash Value Insurance

Cash value insurance refers to a permanent policy, versus term or temporary insurance. It can have a guaranteed level premium, guaranteed death benefit and guaranteed cash value (i.e., equity in the policy) for your life. Four varieties provide the majority of the coverage sold: 1) whole life, 2) universal life, 3) variable life, and 4) variable universal life.

Whole life . Premiums are guaranteed to stay the same for the length of the policy. Your death benefit is guaranteed. You accumulate cash value in the policy but have no say in how the money is invested. The company pays a guaranteed fixed rate of return, and in some cases a dividend as well.

Universal life. The policy's premium payments, death benefits, and cash value build-up are flexible and controlled to a large degree by you. You can adjust the premium deposits and amount of the death benefit over time. In exchange for this flexibility, you share some of the risks, such as mortality costs and investment returns with the insurance company.

Variable life. The investment decisions are made by you, not the insurance company. Premiums are fixed and the death benefit is guaranteed, but the cash value of the policy fluctuates with the performance of the investments you choose. Variable life policies tend to have higher expenses associated with them than do other forms of insurance.

Variable universal life. This product combines the insurance flexibility of universal life with the investment flexibility of variable life in a single insurance product. Variable universal has become a very popular product in recent years due primarily to its flexibility and the unprecedented rise in the stock market. These policies can have as few as four investment options to as many as twenty choices. Pay close attention to the fees that are built in to this product, and keep in mind it is a competitive environment.

Permanent life insurance, as one of its benefits, builds a cash value or equity. Generally, the cash value builds on a tax-deferred basis and, unlike other tax-deferred products, the cash value in your life insurance policy is not subject to the IRS rules regarding distribution prior to age 59½. This a major benefit when life insurance is used as an investment vehicle.

Permanent life insurance allows you to borrow against the cash value portion (but not against the death benefit), usually at favorable interest rates. This isn't to say that it's like a credit card or a revolving line of credit. If you die with a loan balance outstanding, the death benefit is reduced by the amount you owe. Never undertake borrowing from your policy lightly, but know it is there if the need arises.

Term versus Cash Value

Term insurance is appropriate for short-term needs, or when a large benefit is needed and premium dollars are limited for a period of time. Since the premiums increase with age, you can actually pay more money out of pocket for term insurance than for cash value insurance, if you keep it for more than 30 years. Ask your insurance agent for an illustration which shows total premiums paid to life expectancy or beyond, and compare it to the total premiums for cash value insurance.

If you are in a very high tax bracket, the tax advantages of cash value insurance such as variable life may have appeal. As mentioned earlier, this type of policy builds on a tax deferred basis. This feature makes cash value insurance in general, and variable life in particular, an attractive option for regular investors. If finances force you to go the term insurance route, but you expect things might improve later, make sure your term policy has a conversion feature. This way, if you choose to, you can convert your policy to cash value coverage without the necessity of a medical exam. Business, charitable, and estate planning uses of life insurance usually involve permanent policies.

Annuities

There are two basic forms of annuities. A *deferred* annuity permits a single or regular payments into a contract which builds on a tax-deferred basis until some future time. The second form is an *immediate* annuity whereby you make a single payment into the contract and, at some time within the next twelve months, you will begin to liquidate the value of your annuity over an extended period of time. Payments can be guaranteed to be paid for your lifetime, regardless of how long you live, or for a certain period of time only (i.e., 5, 10, 20 years). If someone dies within a short time from when payments began, any balance due would be kept by the insurance company. For this reason many people chose a ten or twenty year guarantee. If they die before the guarantee period, a refund is provided. If they live beyond the guarantee period, they still receive payments, but there is no refund at death.

The money contained in an annuity grows on a tax-deferred basis until it is taken out. Some view annuities as an appropriate technique for managing the risk of outliving their assets, which actually is the original intended use of the product. One drawback to an annuity is the inability to withdraw the money prior to age 59½ without substantial tax and company penalties. This product is most appropriate for such long-term goals as retirement.

Annuities allow gay couples to receive distributions that recognize their potential need to plan for income security over two lives. In contrast, most traditional pension plans offer this benefit only to married couples.

The following characteristics define all annuity contracts:

1. How premiums are paid.

2. When benefits begin.

3. How long benefits are paid out.

4. Who receives the benefits (referred to as *annuitants*).

5. How the annuity grows.

1. How premiums are paid.

Do you make a single payment or a series of payments into your annuity?

You can have a single premium annuity that allows only a one-time payment, or a flexible annuity which allows additional deposits over time.

Annuity contracts generally are written to require one of three payment options:

A)   A *single-premium annuity* requires a payment of one (usually very large) lump sum to fund all future pay-outs. Single-premium annuities are an appropriate choice for someone who is buying an annuity in order to generate a guaranteed income stream (often in retirement), or for someone who wants existing assets designated for retirement use to grow on a tax-advantaged basis.

B)   A *fixed-premium annuity* requires regular periodic payments (monthly, quarterly, or annually) over an extended period of time in order to fund future benefits. Fixed-premium annuities are more desirable for people who want to save on a regular basis.

C)   A *flexible-premium annuity* allows you to alter the amount of the periodic premium in order to best meet your saving and investment goals.

2. When benefits begin.

If you purchase a deferred annuity, you can choose from many options to liquidate. If you purchase an immediate annuity, payments usually begin within 12 months.

When you buy an annuity, you have two choices:

A)   *Immediate annuities* provide for pay-outs to begin as soon as the premium is received. This is a good choice if you are seeking a secure retirement income stream.

B) *Deferred annuities* begin paying out benefits at a future date. This is a good choice for both investment and retirement purposes.

3. How long benefits are paid out.

Usually you will have the choice of several payout options. You may choose a total liquidation in the form of a lump sum, or payments over any number of years. This can be measured in one of four ways:

A) A *pure-life annuity* pays out over the life of the annuitant or over joint lives if there's more than one annuitant. Part of your annuity is used to pay the insurance company's mortality costs. This means you could receive a lower payment in exchange for a guaranteed income for life.

B) A *life annuity with a refund feature* guarantees continued payments for a specified period of time (usually 5, 10, or 20 years), even if the annuitant dies before the payout period ends.

C) An annuity for a certain period guarantees payments for a specified period, usually 5, 10, or 20 years. *Period certain annuities* offer people the ability to plan a retirement income stream while avoiding the need to pay for the insurance company's mortality charges.

D) Most annuities permit the option of withdrawing the entire proceeds in one lump sum. They can enjoy the advantages of tax-deferred build-up during the accumulation period but don't have to bear the insurance company's administration and mortality expenses when the time comes for a payout.

4. Who receives benefits?

With an annuity, you can name a beneficiary and a joint annuitant. You have the option to take the payout over a single life or over the lives of two individuals. Although you may pay your annuity premiums yourself, you have several choices regarding who gets to receive benefits under the contract:

A) An *individual annuity* pays benefits over the life of one person. These annuities are appropriate for single people with no dependents whose primary goal is to guarantee an income stream only for themselves.

B) A *joint-life annuity* pays benefits over the joint lives of (usually) two annuitants. After the first of the joint annuitants dies, the payments stop. These annuities generally don't offer the retirement income protection sought by most couples.

C) A *joint and survivor annuity* also pays benefits over the lives of (usually) two annuitants, but the payments continue until both annuitants die. This feature provides the maximum income security for couples seeking such protection in their retirement years. Remember, however, that promising payments over two lives increases significantly the insurance company's mortality exposure. Joint and survivor annuities therefore offer lower benefits than most other options.

5. How the annuity grows.

You have the choice of a fixed rate guaranteed return or a variable annuity with your dollars invested in a mutual fund like "sub-accounts."

The money you pay into an annuity, whether all at once (as in an immediate annuity) or over time (as with fixed-premium and flexible premium annuities), can grow in one of two ways:

A *fixed-rate annuity* grows at a rate of return projected in the contract. The insurance company is under tremendous pressure to perform consistent with its projections. Therefore, this rate is usually very conservative. These annuities are generally inferior growth-investment vehicles but acceptable for generating an income stream, in retirement.

A *variable-rate annuity* performs (grows or shrinks) based on the return earned by the financial vehicles in which it is invested. Variable annuities, therefore, offer both the risks and the rewards of participating in market-oriented investments. Consequently, the potential return on a variable annuity generally is greater than the return offered by a fixed-rate annuity.

Uses of Annuities

The major advantage to annuities as an investment vehicle is the lure of tax-deferred build up of interest, dividends, and capital gains. This lure is far greater with variable annuities than with fixed-rate annuities.

Using annuities as a means of securing a guaranteed retirement income stream is a less beneficial strategy. Why not invest your money as you see fit, enjoying wider investment choices and the probability of higher returns than most annuities can provide? You then either can withdraw the money from your own investment accounts, on your own schedule, as you need it or want it yourself, making periodical withdrawals over your life expectancy. When you buy an annuity, part of your investment goes to pay the insurance company's administrative costs (and profits). By managing your own money, you avoid these expenses as well as potential mortality charges. On the other hand, if you are bad at managing money, or if you are concerned about the economic security of someone else, using an annuity to guarantee an income stream can make good sense.

Buying an Annuity

With fixed-rate annuities, be skeptical of unrealistic projections. Select only a top-rated company. Be sure that the comparisons you make between companies and products are apples to apples so that all of the key assumptions and variables in the projections are identical.

Be sure that you understand how the insurance company's *surrender charges* work. If you surrender (i.e., cancel) an annuity too soon after opening it, the company will hit you with a penalty known as a surrender charge. Most annuities impose surrender charges only for the first seven to ten years. Usually the surrender charges decrease on a sliding scale over this period. Avoid the rare annuities where the surrender charges never phase out.

If you enter into an annuity contract and then surrender it prematurely, you have to pay income tax on all the deferred build-up. In addition, if you are under 59½, when you surrender your annuity you are subject to a 10% penalty tax imposed by the IRS.

Regarding variable annuities, remember that you must consider both the performance of the insurance company as an insurer and the performance of its separate accounts as investments. Poor investment performance or limited investment options cannot be justified by the lure of tax-deferred savings. Next, make sure the annuity offers at least 5 different investment options, so you can be sure your money is properly diversified. Many variable annuities offer up to twenty different investment options. Lastly, make sure that the total annual fees charged by the insurance company for managing the investments in the variable annuity are reasonable. Generally, fees over 2% are too high and should be avoided.

Disability Insurance

Your most valuable asset is your ability to produce income. A study reported by the American college of life underwriters found that at age 35, an individual faces a one-in-three chance of experiencing total disability for at least three months before age 65, and that nearly 30 percent of those cases result in permanent disability. If you are young and in good health, disability is a greater risk for you than any other hazard, including death.

There are three possible sources for insuring against the risk of disability:

1. State workers compensation insurance for disabilities arising on the job.

2. Social security disability benefits.

3. Disability insurance policies.

What to Look For in a Disability Insurance Policy

1. **Amount of coverage.** Usually this is limited to 60%–70% of your current earned income.

2. **Definition of disability.** Make sure your policy does not exclude "occupational" disabilities. The usual definition of disability is: The inability to perform the material and substantial duties of your occupation.

3. **Definition of occupation.** The best definition is called "own occupation." This means that if you are unable to perform the material and substantial duties of "your occupation," then you are disabled. For example, if you are a surgeon and for some reason you can no longer perform surgery but you could teach, you would still be considered disabled. Others require you to be unfit for work in any occupation; under such, if you take the previous example of the surgeon, if he is able to teach, he would not meet the definition of disability and payments would stop.

4. **Renewability.** Make sure your insurance is non-cancelable or guaranteed renewable. This avoids the risk that your insurer could refuse to renew your policy

at a time when you would be unable to obtain replacement coverage. A policy that is both non-cancelable (meaning as long as you pay the premium you can not be canceled) and guaranteed renewable (meaning your premiums cannot increase) is the best, but can be hard to find.

5. **Waiting period.** This refers to how long you have to wait after becoming disabled before benefits begin to pay. The most common waiting period is 90 days. The longer the waiting period, the lower the premium. Keep in mind, a 90 day waiting period means your first check will come after 120 days. The period before benefits begin is 90 days, and benefits would be paid out about one month later.

6. **Inflation.** Your policy should include a cost-of-living adjustment so that any benefit payments that last over an extended period can keep pace with inflation. There is an extra cost for this benefit, but it provides a larger benefit over time in the event of disability.

7. **Waiver of premium.** Unless your policy includes a provision waiving the continued payment of insurance premiums in the event of a disability, you would have to use part of your disability benefits to keep up the premium payments on your policy. This is a standard feature but you should make sure your policy offers it.

8. **Preexisting conditions.** Benefits can be denied for an illness contracted before the policy begins—even if its existence is unknown. So make sure your policy covers illnesses when they are first manifest, not when they are first contracted or begin.

Health Insurance

The vast majority of Americans receive health insurance coverage as a fringe benefit from their employer. There are two types of coverage common in America: *Comprehensive Major Medical Plans* and *Managed Care Plans.*

Comprehensive Major Medical Plans

There is a wide variety of coverage offered by the various major medical plans. It's important to read your policy, and for some I may as well be asking you to read a dictionary. So, let me just focus on the highlights on which you'll want to focus:

Exclusions. This is a section that requires careful reading because health insurers are drafting increasingly expansive lists of exclusions into their policies. For example, almost all policies exclude coverage for experimental treatments.

Preexisting conditions. This clause generally excludes coverage for a stated period of time (usually six to twelve months) for medical conditions that are already being treated (or already should be under treatment) when the policy begins. Many states have now outlawed this practice and have forced health insurance companies to waive preexisting condition clauses on group policies. This can really be a problem for those with chronic illnesses (e.g., asthma or diabetes) who switch insurance companies when they switch jobs. Sometimes, it makes sense for people to continue purchasing a coverage under their old plan until the preexisting conditions period under their new plan passes. This is done by exercising so-called COBRA rights. I'll explain this later at the end of this section.

Utilization review. This a requirement set up by insurance companies to require the insured to check with the company before undergoing certain medical procedures. The purpose of this requirement is to control medical costs.

Utilization reviews take one of two common forms. Under the first form, *re-certification,* the policyholder must obtain prior approval from the insurance company for any hospital stay or surgical procedure.

Failure to obtain re-certification can result either in a denial of benefits or in benefits being reimbursed at a lower rate. Emergencies usually are excluded from this requirement, although policies containing this form of utilization review generally require policyholders to notify their insurers within 24 hours of an emergency hospital admission.

Case management is the second form of utilization review. It involves the assignment of an insurance company employee to "manage" the treatment of cases involving serious and expensive illnesses, such as cancer or AIDS.

Reimbursement amounts. For a given procedure, the insurance company reimburses their clients. These fees are determined through surveys and other forms of research. The fees a company will permit are then set out in its *usual, customary, and reasonable (UCR)* fee table. Any fees a policyholder incurs in excess of the amount in the UCR table generally are not reimbursed by the company. Make certain these tables are set at a local level, so reimbursement rates are appropriate for a policyholder's geographic location. Reputable insurance companies try to keep their UCR tables current and competitive.

Maximum benefits and policy limits. Many policies specify a lifetime maximum on the amount of benefits they will pay out. Often, this amount is very high (e.g., $2-million), often a low limit may be inadequate to meet the full cost of a very serious illness. Some policies also specify lower limits that apply to particular medical treatments. For example, a policy with a $2-million maximum benefit may also specify a separate $50,000 limit on the expenses associated with rehabilitation treatment programs for alcoholism or drug dependency. Some insurance companies also write lower policy limits for specific illnesses such as AIDS. You should look for a policy with a minimum lifetime benefit amount of at least $2-million and as much as $5-million. And always avoid a single disease policy, such as a "cancer" policy.

Deductibles. This is the amount an individual must pay before they become eligible for any benefits under the policy. One purpose of the deductible is to prevent policyholders from filing small or insignificant claims. A more important purpose of a deductible in the context of health insurance is to encourage policyholders to exercise financial discipline in purchasing medical services. Higher deductibles generally result in lower premiums, so consider a higher deductible if you're looking for ways to keep down the cost of your coverage.

Coinsurance. Many policies require that the person insured pay 20% of the cost of covered services, while the insurance company pays the other 80%. Some policies have even lower coinsurance provisions, meaning policyholders have to pay even more out of their own pockets. A few policies do not require any coinsurance payments. Keep in mind that the coinsurance is payable in addition to the deductible. As an example: If you have $10,000 in medical expenses and you have a typically 80/20 coinsurance with a $1,000 deductible, your out-of-pocket cost would be $2,800, (i.e., $1,000 + [20% x $9,000] = $2,800).

Stop-loss limits. This is a provision that basically says that after you incur x dollars in covered annual medical expenses, the insurance company won't require you to pay any more money for covered medical expenses for the rest of the year. Don't confuse stop-loss limits with maximum benefits provisions. A *stop-loss limit* specifies when you get to stop paying your deductible and coinsurance portion for the year. *Maximum benefits* refers to when the insurance company gets to stop paying for good.

Coordination of benefits. This ensures that the insured does not come out ahead as a result of receiving benefits from more than one source. If you are covered by more than one health insurance plan (perhaps because a spouse or domestic partner also has coverage), the plans usually compare notes to make sure you don't receive back more that 100% of what you paid out in medical expenses.

Supplemental coverage. Comprehensive major medical policies may or may not cover the cost of prescription drugs. They generally do not cover dental or vision care. For many people trying to stretch scarce insurance dollars, prescription drug coverage will represent a better investment than either dental or vision coverage.

Managed Care

Health Maintenance Organization (HMO)

HMO's are an increasingly popular way of obtaining health insurance coverage. In exchange for a monthly fee, the HMO promises to provide an array of medical services in a contract that contains many of the same terms and conditions used in comprehensive major medical plans.

However, there are important differences. HMO's offer the services of only the health care providers who participate in their plans. If a policyholder chooses to seek treatment outside the plan, the expenses generally are not reimbursed. On the plus side, HMO's frequently provide broader coverage for preventive care. The other major advantage of HMO's is that, since they have a greater ability to control costs, the fees they charge their policyholders can be considerably less than those paid for major medical coverage.

On the downside, HMO's limit a policyholder's choice of health care providers to those within its system. Also, some HMO's require you to see a generalist before getting an appointment with a specialist, even when it's painfully apparent that you need specialized treatment. There is a trend now in HMO organizations to allow the patient to self-refer to a specialist. Just make sure yours allows that privilege.

There are two types of HMO's. Under the first type, the health care professionals are all employees of the organization. This is referred to in the health care field as the *Staff Model HMO*, and it's the type of organization most of us think of when we hear the acronym HMO. The other type of HMO, the *Independent Practice Association* (IPA), involves groups or networks of non-affiliated health care providers who have all agreed to abide by the terms of the HMO contract. IPA's tend to give consumers more flexibility in choosing health care providers than do Staff Model HMO's.

Preferred Provider Organizations

PPO's are seen by some people as the health insurance industry's response to the increasing popularity of HMO's. PPO's function largely like major medical policies, containing most of the same features described earlier in this section. However, there are a few additional features.

In a PPO, the insurance company organizes a network of health care providers, much like the IPA-model HMO. Health care providers within the PPO network negotiate reduced fees with the insurance company administering the PPO in exchange for rapid payment and the advantage of being on the preferred provider list. When a policyholder goes to a provider within the PPO network, he or she pays only a nominal coinsurance amount (usually a flat fee of $10 to $20), and is not required to submit any paperwork to the insurance company. In theory, the insurance company benefits from controlled costs, the health care provider benefits from being in the network, and the policyholder benefits from lower premium and coinsurance payments.

One drawback to the PPO arises when the policyholder wants to go outside the network. Usually, the coinsurance percentage payable by the policyholder is higher for out-of-network services. For example, a $10 coinsurance requirement for a visit to an in-network physician could turn into a 30% co-payment for services outside the network. Another drawback is the PPO's, like major medical plans, tend to be less generous with preventive care benefits than HMO's.

Shopping for Insurance

If you are not lucky enough to have insurance through your employment, contact a trade or professional association that represents your line of work. If that doesn't work, consider a local civic or business league or community organization. Sometimes these groups also sponsor plans. Next, request a high deductible when buying insurance. If you increase the amount of the expense you're willing to bear, the insurance company will decrease the amount of money it charges you. Remember to insure against catastrophic losses first, and prioritize the coverage you want. As we saw above, prescription drug coverage is often a smarter insurance buy than vision or dental care. Finally, if affordable coverage still remains elusive, consider going the HMO route. HMO's generally are more cost-effective than private insurance plans and often will contract directly with the general public.

Supplementing Inadequate Coverage

First contact your employee benefits department to find out if it's possible to purchase supplemental coverage yourself. There's a small chance something you don't know about may be available.

Next, consider the HMO option. Generally, your employer is required to offer you the option of an HMO. You will find that you are able to get broader coverage from an HMO than through a private insurance plan.

The final strategy, while technically not insurance, is an important way of controlling health care cost. The tax law allows employers to offer employees, through *cafeteria plans,* the option of setting aside a certain amount of their salaries on a pretax basis to be used for out-of-pocket medical expenses. These plans are usually called Flexible Spending Accounts, or Medical Spending Accounts (MSA). You simply ask the people administering your MSA to reimburse you from your own funds. The expenses paid out of an MSA effectively are subsidized by Uncle Sam, lowering your overall health care costs. The disadvantage of these accounts is that if there's any unspent money left in them at the end of the year, it's forfeited—so plan carefully. Usually, forfeited funds go to a charity designated by the employer.

These accounts are an important way to save on health care.

Continuing Benefits
When You Leave Your Job—COBRA

A federal law known as COBRA requires your employer to permit you to continue purchasing insurance at your own expense for 18 months after you leave, regardless of whose decision it was for you to go. In certain situations, the COBRA period extends for up to 36 months.

COBRA benefits are important for two reasons. First, they can be an excellent source of interim health insurance coverage for people between jobs, or for entrepreneurs striking out on their own. Second, COBRA benefits are an important way for people with chronic and expensive medical conditions to maintain health insurance coverage when switching jobs. Keep in mind most states outlaw the practice of preexisting condition clauses on group health policies. This means that if you change employers and your new employer offers group health, you cannot be declined for coverage or benefits. Check your state for details.

Domestic Partner Benefits

Most, but not all, employees who receive health insurance as a fringe benefit are also offered coverage for their family members. The definition of "family," until recently, never contemplated the alternative family structures established by lesbians and gay men. Experts familiar with the employee benefits area expect that the trend toward domestic partner benefits for lesbian and gay employees will grow in the years ahead, just as it has for unmarried straight families

Because coverage for domestic partners is so new, there is no standard procedure to qualify for domestic partner benefits. Most employers require employees seeking domestic partnership benefits to sign a declaration indicating that the person they seek to cover is in fact a "domestic partner" (however the employer chooses to define that term). The employer may require a house or a joint checking account as proof of a relationship. After these requirements are met, coverage usually begins immediately, subject to much the same terms and conditions as any other employee.

Health Insurance after 65

There are four key components of post-retirement health insurance:

1. **Medicare**, the government-sponsored retiree health insurance program that provides the basis of all retirement health coverage.

2. **Medi-gap policies**, which attempt to fill in some of the gaps in the coverage Medicare provides.

3. **Long Term Care coverage**, specifically excluded from both Medicare and Medi-gap insurance, which is intended to protect against the high financial costs of nursing home or similar care.

4. **Medicaid**, which offers public assistance for seniors of limited means who cannot afford to supplement their Medicare coverage.

No single piece will likely be adequate to meet all your needs. Some of these coverages are certain to be in your arsenal, and it's important for you to understand the basic functions of each coverage.

Medicare

Medicare is a government-sponsored program providing near-universal health care coverage for Americans over age 65 who qualify for Social Security benefits.

Medicare provides health insurance coverage through two separate programs: Part A and Part B.

Part A provides hospital insurance coverage, including benefits for in-patient hospital care, skilled nursing care, home health care, and hospice care. However, there are limits on how much Part A pays for each of these services, as well as for how long they are covered.

Part B provides supplemental medical insurance for a variety of health-related services.

Services not covered by Medicare include long-term custodial care for people who need help with the so-called activities of daily living (ADL's) such as eating, dressing, and bathing; experimental drugs and medical procedures; treatment outside the country; and any procedure Medicare doesn't consider "reasonable and necessary." You either must obtain additional insurance coverage for these services, or pay for them yourself. Anyone who qualifies for Social Security benefits automatically qualifies for Medicare Part A, assuming he or she applies within the time period. You will also qualify for Part B, however, Part B requires an additional premium.

Medi-gap Policies

These policies are privately sold insurance policies intended to fill in the gaps in the health insurance coverage provided by Medicare.

There are 10 types of standardized Medi-gap policies sold, and they are labeled A through J.

Medi-gap plan A picks up the part A hospital coverage and the part B coinsurance expenses that Medicare doesn't pay.

Plans B through J offer various combinations of optional coverage for expenses, ranging from paying Medicare's deductible requirements where they're imposed, and paying the coinsurance on skilled nursing facility expenses, to covering foreign travel emergencies and paying for preventive medical care.

You should apply for Medi-gap coverage at the same time you elect coverage under Medicare part B. If you apply within six months of your part B eligibility, insurance companies are required to sell you the plan (A-J) you want, even if you have health problems that put you in a high-risk category. If you wait more than six months, the insurance company can deny you coverage altogether if you have a preexisting condition.

Long Term Care Insurance

Long Term Care (LTC), or "nursing home" insurance, was developed in response to consumer request to fill the need to help cover the increasing costs of long-term custodial care.

In traditional families, caring for the elderly or ill relatives usually fell on the shoulders of female family members, usually the daughter or daughter-in-law. With the majority of women working today, most no longer have the ability to directly provide the long-term care of a loved one. In the gay community, as with so many other aspect of our lives, we may not have the family unity on which to rely for this support. Therefore, Long Term Care coverage is even more necessary to provide the dignity of choosing how we live out our lives in the event of a terminal or prolonged illness.

According to the National Association of Insurance Commissioners (NIAC) study, 40% of Americans will spend some time in a long-term care facility prior to their death. The average stay in an LTC facility is 4 years, at an average cost in today's dollars of $40,000 per year. Where will this money come from? Nationally, one third of all LTC expenses are paid out of pocket by individuals or their families, 50% is paid by Medicaid, which is becoming more restrictive, and the balance by Medicare.

To help manage this risk, several years ago insurance companies developed and began marketing Long Term Care insurance policies. Although experts familiar with the industry predict that policies will likely become more standard in the future, currently there is no federal uniform format for Long Term care policies. However, many states have uniform policy formats which must be met to market the LTC policy in that state. This means that it is up to you to review carefully the information about a policy you are considering and to ask a lot of questions. Some of the newer LTC policies are called "tax qualified" contracts. This means that if you purchase a Tax Qualified LTC policy, the IRS permits you to deduct the premium payment from your income, much like an IRA deduction.

Medicaid

Medicaid is a combined federal and state government program.

Medicaid enters the retirement health insurance picture in two ways. First, individuals of limited means who cannot afford Medi-gap insurance and who qualify based on their limited resources can receive Medicaid coverage for most of their health care expenses not covered by Medicare. Second, Medicaid pays the skilled nursing facility expenses not covered by Medicare or Medi-gap. This is an important coverage, since neither Medicare nor Medi-gap provides any benefits for nursing home care beyond 100 days—so-called long-term care.

Generally, in order to qualify for this combined federal and state government program, both your assets and your income must be below very limited levels set by your state. While this varies by state, the assets Medicaid will permit you to own and still qualify for coverage are likely to be:

1. Your house, regardless of its value.

2. Your household goods, up to about $2,000 (although most states don't check too carefully).

3. Your car, up to about $5,000.

4. A burial plot, up to about $2,000.

5. Life insurance, up to about $1,500.

6. Between about $15,000 and $80,000 in other assets, known as *exempt resources* (the exact amount is set by your state and indexed for inflation each year).

If your assets are too high to qualify, you must wait until they've been "spent down" in order to receive Medicaid coverage.

Financial advisors realized that their clients could qualify for Medicaid benefits if they artificially spent down their assets, gave them away to friends and family. This is accomplished by a document known as a Medicaid Qualifying Trust (MQT). In an MQT, a person gives up control of their assets to the trust. The assets are distributed much as they would be under your will when you die. Obviously, this is a very scary option for some, but when faced with the grim reality of long-term nursing home costs, increasing numbers are going the MQT route. Recent laws make this a questionable approach. Check with an attorney in your state who specializes in elder law issues.

Homeowners Insurance

Loss of your home and its contents can result in emotional and financial devastation. The insurance industry offers six separate forms of homeowners insurance for six separate risks. The risks are:

1. Damage to your dwellings.

2. Damage to other structures on the property (e.g., shed).

3. Damage to contents.

4. Damage for loss of use.

5. Liability for injuries to others.

6. Medical expenses of others and damage to property of others arising on your property.

Condominium Owners Insurance

When you own a condominium, you need to insure its contents for loss or damage. Your Homeowners Association policy will cover the actual structure but everything within the walls is not covered unless you purchase a condo policy.

Renters Insurance

Renters insurance operates much like condo insurance, except that fixtures, walls, and interior systems like plumbing and wiring aren't covered. If you rent an apartment and have a theft or fire damage, the loss of your property will not be covered by your land-lord's policy. You must carry a renter's policy if you want to cover your property.

Automobile Insurance

There are three categories associated with the ownership or operation of an automobile:

1. **Legal liability to others.** This is the portion of an auto policy that is covered by law in most states. If you are sued as result of an accident, this is the area that will cover that liability up to your policy limit.

2. **Physical injury to oneself or other passengers in the automobile.** This is another form of medical insurance. If you already have medical coverage for yourself and family, you can cancel this portion, however, non-family passengers would not be covered.

3. Comprehensive/collision – **Damage to or loss of your vehicle.** This is what pays to repair your car in the event of fire or accident, or replaces it in the event of theft.

Gay Couples and Cars

Joint ownership of an automobile by an unmarried couple may make it harder to obtain automobile insurance, or it may require you to purchase insurance at higher rates. Another reason not to own a car jointly is that there is no point in putting two names on an asset that is essentially a rolling invitation to be sued.

Although joint ownership is an important estate planning tool for gay couples, automobiles are one instance in which the risks don't outweigh the benefits. Keep each car in one person's name.

Strategies for Lesbians and Gays

Regardless of sexual orientation, people tend to underestimate the risk associated with the loss of ability to earn an income.

Remember that the chances of becoming disabled often can be greater for younger people than the chances of dying. For those of us who are not in a long-term relationship, an illness or injury that caused you to be unable to work would be devastating. Especially if you were unable to turn to your family for financial or other support. Whatever assistance you don't get from your family, you'll have to provide for yourself. If you won't have the resources to draw on from a long-term relationship—financial and otherwise—you have got to think about protecting your income stream.

Chapter Four

The Investment Process

The only question with wealth
is what you do with it.

—John D. Rockefeller

Whether we realize it or not, every day of our lives we make investment decisions that impact our financial future. Some do it unconsciously, and probably fail; others have a well-written, planned system.

Let's say you receive a paycheck and put it into your checking account (investment). You pay your rent, monthly bills, and have a little pocket money (for other expenses). If there's any money left at the end of the month, you leave it in your checking account to help pay next month's bills and expenses (short-term savings). What you may not realize is, you've made decisions about your investment goals (your remaining balance), your time horizon (short—month to month), your risk tolerance (low—cannot afford a loss), your desired rate of return (even lower—usually 0% on a checking account), and your portfolio structure (the checking account).

Identifying Investment Goals

It's important to have and identify investment goals. In other words, what are you saving for? Are you saving toward an emergency fund, a new house, retirement, a college education, a special vacation?

When you plan a trip, you probably get a map and chart your course from point A to point B. Investment goals work the same way. Much like a vacation destination, your goals can change, which is fine, but it's essential that you honestly and fully articulate your goals every time you engage in the investment process. Also remember, it is important to quantify your goals in a specific dollar amount and time frames. Saying you want to be rich, or comfortable, is not adequate. How much money do you want, and by when?

Risk

Many people are surprised to learn that every investment carries some form of risk—even investments for which the U.S. Government guarantees the security of the principal. Before selecting an investment, it is critical that you first understand the types of risk involved, and then honestly evaluate your ability to tolerate those risks.

The Nine Possible Sources of Risk

1. Purchasing Power Risk

Inflation risk is another way of thinking about purchasing power risk. The rate of return earned by your investment may not keep pace with the rate of inflation, effectively eroding the value of your investment principal. We normally accept this risk in our daily lives without even thinking about it, just by leaving money in a passbook savings account. This type of investment barely keeps up with inflation before you consider the effect of tax and inflation.

For example: If your investment is earning 5% before tax, and inflation is at 4%, after taxes, your investment return is in the negative range.

- 5% interest minus 4% inflation rate = 1% net growth

- 5% return x 30% tax rate = 1.5% interest lost to taxes

- 1% net growth minus 1.5% tax rate = <.5%> ("< >" means negative rate of return)

2. Interest Rate Risk

There is a chance that an investment's overall return will be affected by a change in interest rates. For example, a bond has an inverse relationship with interest rates. As interest rates rise, the price of the bonds fall, and when interest rates fall, the price of bonds tend to rise.

3. Re-Investment Risk

This arises when the interest and dividends you receive from an investment cannot be reinvested to provide the same rate of return as your initial investment. This situation occurs because market conditions change between the time of your initial investment and the time you try to reinvest the earnings from that investment.

Reinvestment risk also applies to the principal of an investment with a fixed maturity, such as a bond or certificate of deposit. Say you invested in a CD during the high inflation 1970's and earned a 12% return. If interest rates declined to 8% at renewal time, you could not reinvest that money at the same rate.

4. Market Risk or Volatility Risk

This risk refers to the possibility that the value of the particular investment will rise and fall as a result of changes in the overall markets, even though the individual investment has not changed. Broad market levels sometimes rise and fall unexpectedly as a

result of unanticipated economic or political changes such as inflation reports, unemployment claims, or tax law changes.

5. Business or Economic Risk

The sources of business risk can include everything from envi-
ronmental regulation or the availability of skilled labor to the
firm's ability to generate a profit in its industry, and the compe-
tence of its management.

6. Default Risk

This is the risk that a corporation or government agency is
unable to meet its obligations to its bondholders. For example, a
corporation in financial difficulty may be unable to make the
required interest payment to its bondholders, technically placing
it in default. Securities issued by the federal government are widely
regarded as free of default risk because they are backed by the faith,
credit, and taxing power of the U.S. Government. Generally,
investments that present a high default risk must offer higher
interest than current market rates to attract investors. This type of
bond is commonly referred to as a "junk" bond.

7. Liquidity Risk

This is an owner's ability to quickly convert an investment to
cash when needed. There is a greater possibility that a quick liquidation can result in a loss of value. As an example, if you invest in
real estate, there is a chance that at any given time the market conditions could change so you could be unable to sell your property
quickly, or for a profit.

8. Financial Risk

When a business needs to raise money, it can do so in one of
two ways. It can borrow from others, thereby creating debt, or it
can sell ownership interest in the form of stock. Ownership of corporate stock represents equity to the investors. Most corporations
use a mix of debt and equity financing to meet their capital needs.
A company that uses a lot of debt is said to be highly leveraged.

Generally, the greater the leverage, the higher the financial risk will be to the investor.

9. Exchange Rate Risk

Exchange rate risk is the possibility that a change in the value of a foreign currency relative to the value of the U.S. dollar (or whatever your domestic currency may be) will negatively affect the return on your investment. This risk occurs in international investing or when high rollers invest in foreign currency transactions.

Risk Tolerance

If you lie awake at night worrying about an investment, you might want to look at your ability to cope with risk. Every investment involves risk. Remember, there's no such thing as a risk-free investment. The key is to decide how much of which type of risk you can accept, and for how long.

The most intelligent way to deal with risk is to employ techniques that can help you minimize it. These techniques include selecting the right investments, using dividend reinvestment or dollar cost averaging plans, making proper asset allocations, and, most importantly, diversifying.

Diversification

Financial planners and investment advisers spend years studying the ways in which diversification can minimize risk while maximizing returns. Simply, what you need to know is proper diversification lowers risk.

The easiest way for most of us to diversify our risk is through properly selected mutual funds. Most investors simply do not have the resources to properly diversify an individual stock portfolio. This has created the tremendous popularity in recent years for mutual funds. A good rule of thumb to keep in mind is no individual security (stock or bond) should have a value of greater than 4% of your total portfolio value.

As you can see, it would take quite a bit of cash to properly diversify using individual stocks.

One advantage with diversifying your investments is when one investment is down and the others are doing okay, you'll tend to focus on the big picture—the total return of your portfolio. This should add to your peace of mind. As an example, if one stock represents 4% of your portfolio and that stock loses 25%, of it is value, your overall portfolio will decline by only 1%. If that stock lost 50%, your portfolio would only decline by 2%.

Another important aspect of evaluating an investment's risk and your own risk tolerance is the time frame for your investment. Generally, the longer the time frame for an investment, the greater a person's tolerance toward investment risk can be. This is because the impact of risk is greatly minimized over time.

Risk is a game of probabilities. There are no guarantees any investment will be free of every form of risk, or that the probabilities will play out the way they're expected to. If you're tempted to throw up your hands in disgust and stash your money under the mattress, remember that you've just decided to assume the risk that inflation will erode the purchasing power of your hard earned money. Since risk is an integral part of life, the best we can do is understand its causes, know how we'll respond to it, and make well-informed decisions.

Classes of Investments

All investments represent either an equity interest or a debt interest. You either invest for growth (through ownership) or for income (through loaning your money and being paid interest).

Before we begin the process of structuring the "right" portfolio, we first must understand the different types of investments available to us, called *investment classes.*

The reason asset class selection is so vitally important is explained in a recent study by Brinsom, Singer and Beebower in their article "Determinants of Portfolio Performance II, An

Update" which appeared in the May–June 1991 *Financial Analysts Journal*. This study demonstrated that 91.5% of any portfolio's return can be directly traced to the asset class selection, while only 8.5% of the total return is directly related to specific investment selections.

For each of the following asset classes I will provide:

1. A *description* explaining what the investment class is and how it works.

2. A statement about the vehicle's *investment style* (growth, income, or cash/cash equivalent).

3. The *sources of risk* (discussed in the previous section) for the class of investment.

4. The appropriate *return benchmark*, which can be used to measure the current performance of a particular asset against the average performance of all assets in their class.

5. The average *historical rate of return* the class of investment has earned over time.

Benchmarks and historical rates of return can be useful tools for measuring how a particular investment stacks up against its class, but they are not reliable in predicting future returns. I have used various indexes and different time periods, so be aware of the differences. As an example, you may not be able to compare returns on savings accounts to international stocks.

Savings Accounts

Description: Savings accounts are one of the most conservative forms of investments available. While savings accounts are virtually a license for investment disappointment, it continues to maintain the status as the #1 investment vehicle in the U.S.

Investment style: A savings account is a form of cash equivalent investing.

Sources of risk: Purchasing power risk is the main form of risk associated with savings accounts. Over time, the interest earned will be insufficient to enable the principal in the account to keep pace with inflation. This is even worse when income tax is considered.

Return benchmark: There is no universal agreement on a benchmark, but using quarterly fixed income investments (standard savings accounts), the returns would be 4.91% for 5 years ending in 1998, and 5.25% for a 10-year average. An appropriate comparison would be to use the inflation rate as a benchmark. For the same time frames, the Consumer Price Index rose 2.38% for the 5 years up to 1998, and 3.13% for a 10-year average.

Historical rate of return: The Cost Of Living Index for the period from 1930 to 1998 averaged 3.3%, while savings rates for the same period averaged 4.8%. This results in a before tax difference of 1.5%.

Money Market Accounts or Funds

Description: A money market account is a form of savings account which provides limited check writing ability. In exchange for a minimum balance requirement (often $1,000 or $2,000), money markets provide better interest rates than savings accounts. If the minimum balance is not a problem for you, money markets are preferable to traditional savings accounts. Money Market Mutual Funds (MMF), are different from Money Market Accounts (MMA), in that they are issued by an investment company and not subject to the FDIC guarantees. However, most MMF's have a par value fixed at $1 per share. While rare, keep in mind some money market mutual funds may be subject to principal loss.

Investment style: Money markets are cash equivalents.

Sources of risk: Purchasing power risk is the chief source of risk for money markets.

Return benchmark: Money markets probably are best compared to short-term treasury securities (90-day T-bills). Keep in mind, most money markets invest in T-bills. The money market managers must pay their expenses and make their profits before passing any earnings on to you. Money markets, therefore, generally offer slightly lower interest rates than T-bills in exchange for greater liquidity.

Historical rate of return: Approximately 5% over the 10 year period ending in 1998.

Certificates of Deposit

I like to refer to Certificates of Deposit as "certificates of depreciation." The longer you have your money in CD's, the more you risk losing ground to inflation and taxes.

Description: Certificates of Deposit (CD's) are somewhat similar to savings accounts, except you and the bank agree ahead of time to how long they will keep your money and what the rate of the interest will be for the entire term of the investment.

Investment style: CD's are almost always cash equivalent investments, although very long-term CD's sometimes can be considered income investments.

Sources of risk: Purchasing power risk is the chief source of risk, however, for longer-term CD's, reinvestment risk also may arise if rates have changed significantly since the original investment.

Return benchmark: Because interest rates on CD's vary with the length of the investment, it is not possible to point to a single appropriate benchmark. Some general circulation business publications report the most competitive CD's interest rates quoted by banks.

Historical rate of return: Since returns for CD's vary with the length of the certificate, historical data can get complicated. Using 6-month rates, the returns have been 6.4% for a 5-year average, ending in 1998, and 5.5% for a 10 year average.

Treasury Bills

Description: Treasury bills are the short-term debt (less than 52 weeks) of the federal government. They are backed by the full faith and credit of the U.S. government, making them (theoretically) risk-free investments. They are sold in $1,000 increments, with a minimum investment of $10,000.

Investment style: T-bills are the ultimate form of cash equivalent investing.

Source of risk: Purchasing power risk applies as equally to T-bills as to any other cash equivalent investment. However, because of their short duration, as a practical matter this risk exists only for investors who roll over their T-bills year after year.

Return benchmark: T-bill rates are published in most daily newspapers.

Historical rate of return: The 90-day T-bills have returned an average of 7.3% over the 20 year period ending in 1998, 6.13% for the 5-year period ending in 1998 and 5.42% over the 10-year period ending in 1998.

Treasury Notes and Bonds

Description: Treasury notes are the intermediate-term debt (2 to 10 years) of the federal government.

Investment style: Treasury notes and bonds are generally considered to be income investments.

Sources of risk: Interest rate risk is the chief source of risk for intermediate and long-term treasuries, with reinvestment risk a close second. Purchasing power risk also is a significant issue for treasuries with long maturities.

Return benchmark: Treasury note and bond rates are reported in most major business publications.

Historical rate of return: According to Ibbotson Associates, Inc., intermediate-term government bonds returned 8.3% from 1976 through 1996, whereas long-term bonds returned 9.5% over the same period.

Corporate Bonds

Description: A bond essentially is a form of loan agreement between the issuing entity (corporation or government agency) and the bondholder. In exchange for the receipt of a principal sum, the issuer promises to pay interest semiannually (a dividend), usually for the term of the bond, and to return to the bondholder the principal (face value) at the end of the bond's term.

Investment style: Corporate Bonds are income investments.

Sources of risk: Interest rate risk is a significant source of risk for corporate bonds. Reinvestment risk is another source of risk for many bonds, especially for those with a call feature that allows the issuing corporation to redeem the bond prior to its stated maturity. There is also the risk of a default if the issuing company cannot meet its obligations.

Return benchmark: Most of the major brokerage houses publish indexes of corporate bond performance. Lehman Brothers, Soloman Brothers and Merrill Lynch are the more widely used sources.

Historical rate of return: Ibbotson Associates, Inc. reports that the annual rate of return for corporate bonds from 1926 through 1994 was 5.4%. For a less historical (and perhaps more relevant) perspective, Soloman Brothers reports the 10-year average for such investments through 1998 was 10.85%, and the 5-year average was 8.75%.

Municipal Bonds

Description: Municipal bonds are the debt instruments of state and local governments. States issue bonds to fund the operation and construction of roads, schools, parks, etc.

Investment style: 'Munis' are income investments.

Sources of risk: They are similar to corporate bonds. Liquidity risk can be a concern for the bonds of some smaller municipalities.

Return benchmark: Lehman Brothers and Merrill Lynch publish widely used indexes of municipal bond returns. They generally can be found in business publications.

Historical rate of return: According to Lehman Brothers, for periods ending in 1998, municipal bonds returned 6.8% annually for the preceding 5 years, and 7.75% for the preceding 10 years. Remember that these returns usually are not subject to federal (and issuing state, if you live in that state) income tax.

Common Stock

Description: Common stock represents an ownership interest in the company that issued it.

Investment style: Most stocks are growth investments, although some preferred and high-dividend common stocks may be considered income investments.

Sources of risk: Every stock has some degree of risk. It is therefore important to focus on whether the source of risk is significant or insignificant. And yes, it's possible that some day the whole system could come crashing down, making even the most blue-chip of stocks near worthless. If this happens, you'll probably have bigger worries than your portfolio. No investment would survive the apocalypse, including those guaranteed by the U.S. government.

Return benchmark: There is no universal agreement on the appropriate benchmark for establishing the overall performance of the stock market. The Dow Jones industrial average, which is the most widely quoted, tracks only 30 stocks. I do not consider it a good measurement of the overall health of the market. If you want to check the performance of a diverse common stock mutual fund, comparing its 5-year return to that of the S & P 500 or the Wilshire 5000 is an excellent place to start. The S & P 500 is reported in the business section of most daily newspapers. The Wilshire 5000 can be a little harder to find, and you may have to turn to a business publication to get current figures.

Historical rate of return: Ibbotson Associates, Inc. reports that from 1926 through 1998, the U.S. equities market of large corporations posted an average annual return of 12.3%. For more recent periods ending in 1998, the S & P 500 averaged an annual return of 24.02% over the 5-year period, 19.16% going back 10 years, and 17.75% going back 20 years. Similarly, the Dow Jones returned an annual average of 22.27% for the 5 years ending in 1998, and 18.81% for the 10 years ending in 1998.

Preferred Stock

Description: Preferred stock is similar to common stock in that it represents an ownership interest in a corporation. Unlike common stock, it has a "preferred" right to receive proceeds in the event the corporation is liquidated. The good news for investors in preferred stock is the full stated dividend gets paid before investors holding common stock get anything. The bad news for investors in preferred stock is that only the stated dividend gets paid, even if the company's performance is spectacular.

Investment style: Preferred stock is a form of income investing.

Sources of risk: Interest rate, purchasing power, and business risk are the chief sources of risk for preferred stock.

Return benchmark: There is no index that measures the performance of preferred stock.

Historical rate of return: Ibbotson Associates, Inc. reports that the annual rate of return for broad fixed-income investments was 5.4% from 1926 through 1994.

Income Stock

Description: Income stocks are common stocks that consistently pay superior dividends. Generally, it is a function of the industry in which the corporation operates. Because of their lack of relationship to the economic cycle, income stocks are sometimes referred to as defensive stocks.

Investment style: Although it is reasonable to expect modest annual growth from income stocks, they are generally thought of as income investments.

Sources of risk: Income stocks bear most of the risks of common stocks (market, business, and financial), although perhaps to a lesser degree. Investors in income stocks also need to consider interest rate risk.

Return benchmark: There is no single benchmark for income stocks.

Historical rate of return: Using Standard and Poor's 40 Utilities, the returns over the 5 years ending in 1998 was 13.96%, and the 10-year average was 14.58%.

International Stock

Description: These are stocks which represent ownership interests in foreign corporations.

Investment style: International stocks usually are growth investments.

Sources of risk: One form of risk is the exchange rate risk, which is not present with U.S. corporation stock. This is the daily fluctuations of the value of foreign currency against the U.S. dollars. A particular form of business risk may exist in some foreign countries, the risk that a government may nationalize (i.e., take over) an industry or corporation, decimating the value of your investment. Finally, there are liquidity risks associated with obscure foreign stocks, as there may not be a buyer when you want to sell an esoteric issue. Regardless, most investors should have some part of their investment portfolio in international stocks through mutual funds, for diversification.

Return benchmark: Morgan Stanley publishes a widely recognized benchmark for international stocks: MSCI EAFE (EAFE stands for Europe, Australia, and the Far East). It measures the performance of international stocks in the developed countries. The MSCI EAFE is published in most major business publications.

Historical rate of return: The average annual return of the MSCI EAFE for the 5 years ending in 1998 was 11.06%, and for the 10 years ending in 1998 it was 3.9%.

Mutual Funds

The first mutual fund was established in 1924 and, since that time, nearly 10,000 different funds have been established. You can find a mutual fund to meet most any objective and that fits into any of the different asset classes. When you buy shares of a mutual fund you are, in essence, buying a proportional interest in all the investments the fund owns. It would be very difficult for the average investor to achieve this level of diversification through direct purchases.

There are four ways to earn money in mutual fund investments, each paralleling the ways you earn money in direct investments:

1. The fund can distribute your share of its earnings from debt in the form of interest.

2. The fund can distribute your share of its dividend earnings from equity investments.

3. The fund can distribute your share of the capital gain it earns on the investments it sells.

4. The value of your shares can increase as the value of the fund's holdings appreciates.

When considering stock mutual funds, keep in mind most funds distribute earnings to their owners annually, usually in December. Be sure to avoid buying into a stock fund—unless it's part of a systematic investing plan—just before it makes its annual distributions. Since the fund's share price goes down by the amount of the distribution, and the distribution is taxable to you, you pay tax on the money you've just invested if you buy right before the distribution is made. This concern doesn't apply in the case of funds held through tax-advantaged vehicles like retirement plans.

The basic rules of capitalizing on mutual funds is to remember the less a fund charges, the more you keep.

There are three broad categories of fees a fund may charge: sales fees, management fees, and so-called 12 (b) (1) fees. Different funds charge these fees in different combinations, so read the *prospectus* (the descriptive literature the fund provides you) carefully. The applicable fees are spelled out in the fee schedule of the prospectus.

Sales fees, also called *loads*, can be charged when you buy into the fund (front-end loads) or when you withdraw from it prematurely (redemption fees). Also, keep in mind that loads are a one-time charge. Thus, the longer you hold an investment, the less significant the load's impact on your annual return.

Finally, understand if you're working through an investment professional, there's a good chance that part of any sales fee you pay will go into his or her pocket in the form of a sales commission. As Jerry Seinfeld would say, "Not that there is anything wrong with that!" What Jerry is getting at is you don't have to be afraid of paying a commission or load. All mutual funds will have various management fees and expense charges whether or not they charge a load. These costs are usually deducted from the overall fund and are reflected in a reduced rate of return. They are not taken out of your individual account. If you have little investment experience, you may want to look at the load from the perspective of paying a fee for a service. Let's look at how you might see a commission, or load, from the perspective of simply paying a fee for service.

If you are someone who repairs your own car, then you probably wouldn't pay a mechanic to change your oil. If you can do it yourself, and it's something you normally do, why pay someone else? You may have taken classes, read books, played around on your own, or been taught by someone else how to repair a car. Most people I speak with don't repair their own cars. And, none of them take their auto in for repair and expect the mechanic to do it for free. The mechanic has the training, education, and experience to do the repair, and people expect to pay for that.

If you have the education, training and experience to do financial planning, insurance analysis or investment evaluations, then you wouldn't need to use a financial planner, insurance agent or stock broker. If you can do it yourself, you wouldn't need to pay someone else for his or her advice or assistance, unless you still want to have someone confirm your conclusions. You've probably heard the expression, "If a lawyer represents himself (or herself) in court, they have a fool for a client." If you want someone who can provide advice, someone who can ask you questions which will create clarity and provide appropriate recommendations based on your unique situation, then you will need to pay someone either through a fee, or through a commission from the products they sell. Many financial planners and insurance agents will work with you for only the commissions they will receive from the products you buy. This can be an easy, nearly painless way to get advice and pay for their services.

Usually, no-load funds have higher management fees than funds which charge a load. The reasons deal with the level of advertising and staffing needs required. A fund which charges a load must offset the costs paid to the financial planner or stock broker up front. Since the costs are paid up front, the fund can reduce their ongoing management fees.

If you were to compare two mutual funds, one with a load and low management fees, and the other with no load and the typically higher management fees, your total expenses would be less with the load fund after 4–6 years.

The prospectus is a document which is required to be provided to you, under current law, and contains the information the Securities and Exchange Commission feels every investor ought to have. This will contain all the information on fees and expenses. Always read the prospectus, and if you don't understand what it says, have it explained to you.

There are many objectives you can pursue through mutual fund investing—blue chip companies, small capitalized companies, utilities, growth, aggressive growth, and more. The following are a few of those:

Value Funds

Description: Value funds seek growth by investing in common stocks that the fund's analysts have identified as undervalued by the market. The fund's managers try to provide superior returns by identifying and investing in undervalued companies.

Investment style: Value funds are a growth investment.

Sources of risk: Given the nature of value investing, the level of these risks may be above average.

Return benchmark: There is no identifiable benchmark for value stocks or value funds.

Historical rate of return: There is no historical return data specific to value stocks.

Aggressive Growth Funds

Description: Aggressive growth funds are basically stock funds. The stocks are usually of smaller companies or in an industry which is expected to have rapid growth.

Investment style: Aggressive growth funds are a form of growth investing.

Sources of risk: The sources of risk are those typical to stock funds—market, business, and financial risk. However, each of these risks is magnified by the nature of aggressive growth investing. Keep in mind, a substantial part of investment risk is simply avoided by time in the market. Therefore, aggressive growth investments are best purchased for long-term goals, such as retirement many years from now.

Return benchmark: There is no widely available benchmark for aggressive growth stocks.

Historical rate of return: Morning Star reports for the 5 years ending in 1994, aggressive growth funds had an average annual return of 11.1%, and for the 10 years ending in 1994, the return was 13.4%.

Small Capitalization Funds

Description: Small capitalization funds invest in new ventures under the theory the greatest potential for long-term growth exists there. Small Cap stocks are generally companies with market capitalizations of less than one billion dollars. Because small cap companies are usually start-up ventures, it's highly unlikely they'll pay dividends for many years.

Investment style: Small cap funds are growth investments.

Sources of risk: The sources of risk are those typical to stock funds—business, financial, and market risk. However, each risk is magnified by the nature of small cap investing.

Return benchmark: Although a precise benchmark for small caps is hard to find, two contenders come very close; the NASDAQ composite index, and the Russell 2000.

Historical rate of return: Through 1998, the Russell 2000 averaged 12.27% over 5 years and 13.97% over 10 years.

International Stock Funds

Description: International stock mutual funds offer average investors exposure to a wide variety of foreign investment options. These can range from diversified funds to funds that limit their investments to a particular region or country, such as European Funds, Pacific Rim Funds, or Emerging Market Funds.

Investment style: Usually growth investments.

Sources of risk: The sources of risk for diversified international funds are the same as those for direct international investments. Your investment is captive to the overall economic performance of a given country or region. Moreover, in emerging markets, significant political risk and other forms of business risk not familiar to U.S. investors are a source of concern.

Return benchmark: The MSCI EAFE discussed above is an appropriate benchmark for diversified International Funds. Lipper also computes and provides many indexes, among them are those appropriate to regional or country funds. These include the Europe, Pacific and Japan Indexes.

Historical rate of return: For periods ending in 1998, the 5-year average return for Europe was 16.66%, for the Pacific it was –7.08% (negative return), and for Japan it was 10.6%.

Sector Funds

Description: Sector Funds offer investors who believe a particular industry or region the opportunity for superior growth to concentrate their investments within that area.

Investment style: Usually growth investments. However, some sector funds (e.g., utility funds) have an income element to them.

Sources of risk: All the sources of risk common to stock investments apply to sector funds. However, the sector portfolio is more tied to the fortunes of a particular industry or region than a broad market portfolio.

Return benchmark: Information by sector is very hard to come by. The major analytical services compile data for some of the more popular sectors.

Historical rate of return: The broad market returns may be a good starting point for gauging the performance of sector funds.

Real Estate

Description: Investors can own real estate either directly or indirectly. Forms of direct ownership include a primary residence, a vacation home, vacant land, residential rental property, and commercial property. Indirect ownership usually comes in the form of either a Real Estate Investment Trust (REIT), or a Real Estate Limited Partnership. The appeal of owning real estate is its ability—usually—to provide an effective hedge against inflation, and that appeal has proven considerable over time. On the other hand, direct owners assume all the costs and headache incident to ownership, the risk investment property will not appreciate, and the risk property intended to produce income will not do so.

REITS are real estate investments which trade like stocks and work somewhat like mutual funds. Real estate limited partnerships allow a small group of investors to band together and directly own a particular property or small number of properties, such as a shopping center.

Investment style: Real estate investments are growth vehicles, except for mortgage REITS, which are income investments.

Sources of risk: The chief sources of risk for real estate are significant liquidity risk and market risk.

Return benchmark: Consult a knowledgeable professional or public library in the area where the property is located.

Historical rate of return: The advisory firm of Callan Associates, Inc. reports that, through 1994, the composite return of real estate investments of all types was 8.1% over 20 years, 3.6% over 10 years, and -0.6% over 5 years.

Aggressive Investments

For the average investor, commodities, futures and options are tantamount to playing the lottery. Or, for those with deep pockets and nerves of steel, commodities and options can be minor players in your portfolio.

Futures: A *futures contract* is an agreement made in the present to buy and sell specific commodities (rice, wheat, soybeans, etc.) at a stated price on a stated date in the future.

Options: An *option* gives the holder the right to decide whether or not to buy or sell a specified stock (or futures contract) at a specified price (called the *strike price*) before the option expires. A *call* is the right to buy a specific stock at the strike price. A *put* is the right to sell the stock at the strike price. Speculators who expect the price of a stock to change can make handsome profits if they are right, and lose big if they are wrong.

Asset Allocation and Portfolio Structure

Now that you have an understanding of the various classes of investments, you've reached the critical phase of the investment process: selecting the investment vehicles appropriate for your goals, time frames, and risk tolerances. Generally, it would behoove you to make these financial decisions with a professional. The task is daunting, and the truth is most people simply do not have the necessary ability or time to sift through the reams of investment data that financial planners, investment advisers, brokers, or other professionals do.

Asset Allocation

By now you should also understand that portfolio diversification is one of the cornerstones of the investment process. Diversification doesn't mean just putting your eggs in several baskets, it means putting them in several kinds of baskets by investing in more than one class of assets.

Let's consider several possible allocations based on the time horizon for the underlying investment goals.

Long-term Investment Goals

If your time frame for investing involves long-term goals, you need to first focus on growth, next on income, and finally on what is traditionally referred to as security of principal. For our purposes, long-term generally means 10 years or longer. Retirement portfolios are the most common examples of long-term investments—at least for those under age 55. An investor with long-term goals and average risk tolerance might consider allocating about 60% of their portfolio to growth vehicles, about 30% to income vehicles, and about 10% to cash and cash equivalents.

Intermediate-term Investment Goals

Intermediate term goals range from 5 to 10 years. Saving for a child's college education is a common example. An investor with intermediate-term goals and average risk tolerance might consider allocating 40% of their portfolio to growth vehicles, 40% to income vehicles, and 20% to cash and cash equivalents. Again, variations of plus or minus 5% to 15% are common.

Short-term Investment Goals

Short-term investing normally involves a time frame of less than 5 years. Saving for a down payment on a house, a new car, or a special vacation are good examples of short-term investment goals. An investor with this type of goal should consider very stable, fixed type of investments such as savings, money markets, or CD's.

Current Income Goals

People living in retirement are a common example of investors with current income goals, although anyone who must rely on their investments for a current income stream fits in this category. Thus, an investor with current income goals and average risk tolerance ought to consider allocating 20% of their portfolio to conservative growth vehicles, 50% to income vehicles, and 30% to cash or cash equivalents. Allocation recommendations can vary by plus or minus 5% to 15%. This will allow you to have some hedge against inflation in the future.

Allocating Retirement Savings

Regardless of whether your goal for retirement savings is long, intermediate, or short-term, some financial planners recommend as a general rule the percentage of your retirement assets allocated to income and cash (combined) shouldn't exceed your age. It is still important to have a portion of your portfolio allocated for growth.

As an example, according to this theory, if you are 35 years old, the portion of your assets allocated to income and cash should not exceed 35%. When you are age 50, it should not exceed 50%. Figuring risk into the mix, if your risk tolerance is average, the allocations described above may be appropriate for you. As a general rule, if your risk tolerance is high, you'll want to adjust the allocations to favor growth more, and both income and cash less. If your risk tolerance is low, you'll want to do the reverse—increase the allocations to both cash and income, and decrease the allocation to growth. Sometimes, if an adjustment from cash to growth (or vice versa) seems too extreme, allocation adjustments to favor income can be a good compromise.

Accommodating Multiple Goals

Many investors intend for their portfolio to achieve more than one investment goal. For example, you may be trying simultaneously to save for retirement and for the down payment on a house. If you find yourself in this common situation, it may be helpful to think of your portfolio in separate segments. In this way, you will create one set of allocations for your long-term goals, another for your short-term goals, and so on. This is especially important when one of your goals is for retirement since, most of the time, the funds allocated in retirement accounts are not accessible without substantial penalties.

Allocating Within Each Investment Style

To prepare for this next step, we need to review the investment styles of the various investment classes from which we will eventually choose. Here's a quick review of the information presented in the previous section's discussion of investment classes (excluding the aggressive investment).

Growth investments: These include common stocks, (most) international stocks, directly owned real estate, equity REITS, real estate limited partnerships, and mutual funds whose holdings are comprised of growth investments (including value funds, aggressive growth funds, small cap funds, international and emerging market funds, and sector funds).

Income investments: These include certain long-term certificates of deposit, corporate bonds, municipal bonds, treasury notes and bonds, preferred stocks, some high-dividend stocks (e.g., utility company stock), mortgage REITS, and mutual funds whose holdings are comprised of income investments.

Cash and cash equivalents: These include savings accounts, most certificates of deposit, money markets, and treasury bills. These would be most any type of account where you have ready access to your money.

Allocating Among Growth Investments

Depending on your risk tolerance, you should allocate between 50% and 70% of your growth portfolio to a diversified selection of these stock investments (with lower risk tolerances tending toward the lower end of this range). However, there are other classes of growth investments from which to choose. In small to moderate amounts, they are appropriate considerations for most portfolios. They include small cap, aggressive growth, and/or value stocks, international stocks, and real estate. Average investors should avoid allocating any more than 15% of their growth portfolios to any one of these investment classes. Also, as discussed earlier, limit your assets in any one security to 4% or less. The exception is if you own your own business and the value of your business exceeds 4% of your overall portfolio.

Portfolios with long time-horizons should have at least a small portion of their growth assets invested in small cap and aggressive growth stocks, and, unless your portfolio is very large, probably through mutual funds. Mutual funds with international stocks should be a part of your portfolio because foreign markets don't always follow the domestic markets' ups and downs, which can provide an important balance.

Investing in real estate also could be a part of most growth portfolios. Real estate is thought to be a good long-term hedge against inflation, and some real estate investments offer the possibility of superior returns.

Allocating Among Income Investments

The majority (60% to 80%) of your income portfolio should be allocated to a diversified mix of investment grade corporate bonds, municipal bonds, treasury notes and bonds, and blue-chip preferred stocks.

A general word of caution about investing in bonds is in order. More than a few investors have seen changing interest rates erode the value of their bonds. Bond prices have an inverse relationship to interest rates, which means as interest rates increase, the value of bonds tends to decrease. Generally, long-term bonds (10–30 yr.) will be effected more than short-term bonds. So, if you need to sell your bonds before maturity, and interest rates have increased, the value of your bonds may have gone down substantially.

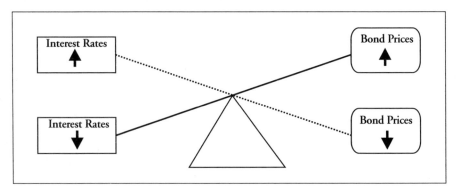

Bond prices have an inverse relationship to interest rates.

Allocating Among Cash or Cash Equivalents

Allocations are made to cash for two main reasons: security of principal and liquidity. Many people appreciate the peace of mind in knowing their money is available and not subject to the ups and downs of the stock market.

Choosing Individual Investments

It is impossible for a book to guide individual investors to precise conclusions. However, we can advise you of some ground rules that can help you structure your individual choices. There is no single set of uniform rules for choosing individual investments, and investors over time will develop their own styles. However, every prudent investor will consider the following in making investment decisions:

1. *Gather data.* Obtain and read the prospectus for any investment you're considering. Find out what changes may be brewing that could affect the company's future performance—management changes, changes in the industry, the economy, and so on. A Los Angeles Times article (April 1999) reported about an elderly widow who lost $900,000 in an investment scheme. She was given no prospectus.

2. *Compare numbers.* Once you've obtained the financial data you need about an investment's past performance, compare it to: A) the other investments you're considering, B) the historical rate of return for that class of investment and, C) the current benchmark return for that class of investment. Be sure that your number comparisons are apples to apples. Many professionals recommend reviewing an investment's 3-year, 5-year, and 10-year average returns in order to make a proper evaluation. Prudent investors always do their homework prior to investing.

3. *Transaction costs.* It costs money to buy and sell most investments—brokerage commissions, mutual fund loads, sales charges, and so on. Many investments also charge annual maintenance fees, custodial fees at banks and brokerage houses. Make sure that the figures you use to compare investments account for all transaction costs associated with the investment.

4. *Past performance is not a complete guide.* We look to the past because it's where most of the analyzable data is, and the data usually tells us some of what we need to know. But the data does not tell us everything, so we

have to turn to what professionals call *fundamental analysis* to finish the job.

Fundamental analysis simply means taking a hard look at the economic fundamentals of an investment. Pertinent questions include:

A) What is the current economic environment, and what impact is it likely to have on the investment?

B) What is the current political/regulatory climate, and what impact is it likely to have on the investment?

C) What changes are occurring in the industry in which the investment operates that might have an impact on its financial performance?

D) For stocks, is the current price supported by the company's earnings (Price Earning Ratio)?

E) For bonds, what is the issuer's creditworthiness? Bonds are rated A, AA, AAA, B, BB, BBB for investment grades. So-called "junk" bonds are rated C, CC, CCC. The lower the rating, the higher the return, also the higher the risk.

F) For mutual funds, what recent changes have occurred (or are rumored to shortly occur) in the fund's management?

5. *Mutual funds or individual issues?* Unless you have a significant amount of money to invest—probably into six figures—you very likely cannot match the diversification offered to you by a mutual fund.

6. *Balanced funds.* They invest some of their portfolio in growth and some in income. But remember that investing in a balanced fund is not a substitute for the diversification strategies.

7. *Index funds.* Index funds attempt to provide returns that match exactly the performance of a given benchmark index. They tend to have slightly lower management expenses than other mutual funds. They also tend to sell their investments less frequently, which means owners have to report fewer capital gains on their tax returns.

8. *Systematic investing.* There are two particular forms of systematic investing:

    A) **Dollar-cost Averaging.** This is a technique wherein you invest a fixed amount at regular intervals. Doing so minimizes the impact of price fluctuations of your investment, in fact, it even takes advantage of the volatility and maximizes return over time. Any new investor into the market should use dollar-cost averaging as a cornerstone investment strategy.

    B) **Dividend Reinvestment Programs (DRIP).** You instruct the entity paying you dividends (usually your stock brokerage or mutual fund) to reinvest the payment in additional shares of the investment. This is usually done at no fee, also called Net Asset Value.

Strategies

Should lesbians and gays give extra consideration to investing in organizations that have made an extra effort to advance our causes? A communications company that bans anti-gay discrimination, a software developer that offers its employees domestic partner benefits, or a rental car company that does not charge domestic partner renters an "additional driver" fee are examples of companies doing right by us.

This question is highly personal; most professional advisers are likely to give a yes and no response. It is certainly appropriate to make social responsibility a consideration in investment decisions, but it is not in your best interest to make it the determining factor. In addition, it is probably much less risky to reject homophobic investments than it is to require all your investments be gay-friendly. Only after an investment makes good financial sense should social criteria come into play.

Remember, the investment process is cyclical and, for a prudent investor, it should never end. You must periodically review your allocations to ensure they are still appropriate to your goals, time frames, and risk tolerance. You must also review your portfolio to ensure the investments you own actually reflect the allocations on which you've decided. For a variety of reasons, the assets in your portfolio will grow at different rates, and you may need to occasionally adjust the composition of your portfolio to be sure it tracks the allocation on which you've settled.

You don't need to be obsessive about your reviews; more than once a year can be counterproductive. On the other hand, if you let your review slide for more than two years, you're probably slacking off. Many mutual funds and brokerage accounts have automated investment strategies that will automatically "re-balance" your portfolio to the original allocations each month, or each quarter. I strongly recommend you take advantage of this feature, if available.

Chapter Five

Computing Retirement Needs and Savings

The great end of life is not knowledge,
but action.

—Thomas Huxley

Think of the retirement planning process as a three-legged stool. One leg is the retirement plan provided by an individual's employer. The other leg comes from Social Security retirement benefits. The third leg is derived from an individual's own savings. The amount of retirement support provided by each leg of the stool varies considerably from person to person. Therefore, it is very important for you to understand what each leg is going to look like on your particular stool. So, our first step in this process is to compute your retirement needs.

The task at first seems simple. Most people need somewhere between 60% and 80% of their pre-retirement income in order to enjoy a comparable lifestyle in retirement. While this may sound high at first, research and experience show it's the way things usually work out. If you think about it for a second, retiring is a lot like going out on disability—at least from the perspective of what it does to your cash flow. If your house is paid for when you retire, you'll be at the low end of this range. If you plan to travel a lot, figure on coming in near the top end.

On a more specific level, however, you need to know not just what your retirement income needs will be, but how much you have to save in order to meet those needs, to build your leg of the stool. Figuring this out is not easy, but it is possible. What makes it so complicated is the number of variables and assumptions that go into the process: When you'll retire, what impact inflation will have on your retirement income needs, what rate of return your nest egg will earn both before and after retirement, and how long you'll live in retirement. This is why the software and the expertise available from professionals and investment institutions can be so valuable. Nevertheless, it can be an instructive exercise to work through the process yourself.

Again, it's only possible to do this if several assumptions are made. If these assumptions prove to be wrong or inappropriate for you, the resulting numbers will be inaccurate for you as well.

As we work through the process, you'll be told the assumptions being made at each step along the way. While the assumptions we make here are common, if they're not right for you, ultimately you'll need a computer, an expert, or both. The figures used in this section have been rounded to keep them manageable. The rounding always has been done erring on the side of caution. In order to keep the computations as conservative as possible, sometimes a three or a four got rounded up instead of down, or a six or seven got rounded down instead of up. Nevertheless, be advised that rounding big numbers over long time frames can have a surprisingly significant impact on the final result. Note, too, that some of the numbers we'll be dealing with may seem surreally large. Many of us will be working with seven-digit figures (as in millions of dollars). No matter how absurd these numbers might seem, rest assured they are very real. Inflation and time are working against you in this regard.

One final warning: Never skip any of the steps in this process. If you decide to change a figure or an assumption, always go back to Step 1 and start again.

With this background, let's begin the process of computing retirement savings needs.

Step 1. Compute annual retirement income needs in today's dollars.

Review your annual budget from Chapter Two and analyze your levels of income and expenses. Consider which expenses are likely to increase and which are likely to decrease when you retire, and determine where you fall in the 60% to 80% range.

Consider that, on the one hand, if your house is paid off, your expenses will tend to be lower. However, the other costs associated with home ownership (property taxes, repairs, homeowners association fees) will go up over time. Next, be sure to factor in the likelihood that your expenditures for health care will increase substantially. Finally, think about the retirement lifestyle you aspire to. Are you the kind of person who will be satisfied with simple, quiet golden years? Or will retirement be the time for you to do all the things you've spent the last 30 years dreaming about? An active retirement will cost more.

Step 2. Subtract annual Social Security benefits estimated in today's dollars.

We treat Social Security retirement benefits separately because they are adjusted each year for inflation (at least under current law). Other common sources of retirement income—employer pensions, annuities and earnings on retirement savings already in place—tend to remain constant throughout retirement (i.e., they generally are not adjusted each year for inflation).

Step 3. Grow annual net needs for inflation.

After determining your annual net income needs in today's dollars, you must grow that figure for inflation. If, for example, you're 25 years old, you know that your income needs when you retire in 40 years will be significantly higher than they are right now due to inflation.

Table 5-1
Inflating Current Needs Into Future Needs

	Years Until Retirement			
Current Needs ↓ Projected future needs per year ➡	40	30	20	10
$10,000	$48,000	$32,400	$21,900	$14,800
$20,000	$96,000	$ 64,900	$43,800	$29,600
$30,000	$144,000	$97,300	$65,700	$44,400
$40,000	$192,000	$129,700	$87,600	$59,200
$50,000	$240,000	$162,200	$109,600	$74,000
$60,000	$288,000	$194,600	$131,500	$88,800
$70,000	$336,000	$227,000	$153,400	$103,600
$80,000	$384,000	$259,500	$175,300	$118,400
$90,000	$432,000	$291,900	$197,200	$133,200
$100,000	$480,000	$324,300	$219,100	$148,000

The table assumes that your current income will grow at 4% per year. If inflation turns out to average more than this amount over time, you will need to save more. The figures have been rounded to the nearest 100.

Step 4. Compute total funds needed at retirement.

In order to compute this step, you will need to make a very critical assumption: How many years you expect to live in retirement. This is probably the hardest assumption in the retirement planning process, when you'll die.

Anticipated Years in Retirement

There are quite a few things to note about this table. First, it assumes that inflation will grow at 4%, and that your investments in retirement will earn 6%. It assumes the income we are projecting for retirement is the same income you're earning now, which has not been adjusted for inflation. Nevertheless, if your actual rate of return is lower, you will need to start out with a larger amount in order to fund the same retirement income needs. If your actual rate of return is higher, which is what we are aiming for, you will need a smaller amount (See *Alternative Method*).

Next, the figures in the table have been rounded to the nearest 100 (using the approximate rounding explained in the beginning of this section). Most importantly, this table assumes that you will consume your savings over the time period you've chosen. In other words, it assumes that you will spend your principal down to zero over the time period chosen.

Alternative Method

Another far more effective approach is to assume you will only live on the earnings of your investment portfolio, and never use the principal. This will do two things for you. One, you won't have to figure out how long you will live, because you're only living on the earnings. And two, the principal can continue to grow to provide higher earnings in the future.

With the advice of a competent financial planner, you can be guided to investments which could provide an income of 8%, 10% or even 12% annually, instead of the 6% used in the tables. The higher the projected return, the lower the principal needed,

Table 5-2
Total Funds Needed At Retirement

Current Annual Need → / Total Funds Needed ↑	Anticipated Years Spent In Retirement				
	15	20	25	30	35
$10,000	$129,200	$164,700	$197,000	$226,400	$253,000
$20,000	$258,500	$329,500	$394,000	$452,700	$506,100
$30,000	$387,700	$494,200	$591,000	$679,100	$759,100
$40,000	$516,900	$658,900	$788,000	$905,400	$1,012,100
$50,000	$646,200	$823,700	$985,000	$1,131,800	$1,265,200
$60,000	$775,400	$988,400	$1,182,100	$1,358,100	$1,518,200
$70,000	$904,600	$1,153,100	$1,379,100	$1,584,500	$1,771,200
$80,000	$1,033,900	$1,317,900	$1,576,100	$1,810,800	$2,024,300
$90,000	$1,163,100	$1,482,600	$1,773,100	$2,037,200	$2,277,300
$100,000	$1,292,400	$1,647,400	$1,970,100	$2,263,500	$2,530,300
$110,000	$1,421,600	$1,812,100	$2,167,100	$2,489,900	$2,783,400
$120,000	$1,550,900	$1,976,800	$2,364,100	$2,716,300	$3,036,400
$130,000	$1,680,000	$2,141,600	$2,561,200	$2,942,600	$3,289,400
$140,000	$1,809,300	$2,306,300	$2,758,200	$3,169,000	$3,542,500
$150,000	$1,938,500	$2,471,000	$2,955,200	$3,395,300	$3,795,500

and the easier it will be to reach your goals. Again, I recommend you seek the advice of a competent financial planner to support you with your specific situation.

Step 5. Subtract other sources of retirement income.

After you know what your total funds needed at retirement will be, you need to account for your employer's leg of the stool—assuming that it exists. In Step 4, you were to compute the total amount of money you would need for retirement based on the level of income you needed or desired. In this step, you subtract the lump sum equivalent of other sources of income, such as an employer's noncontributory pension plan, an annuity, or savings already in place. We account for these items here because they tend to remain constant throughout retirement; that is, they do not increase each year for inflation.

If you already own an annuity, use Table 5-3 to convert the annual annuity payment into a lump sum. (If the insurance company provides you with a lump-sum value, use their figure, and not the one from the table.) Subtract the lump sum from the result of Step 4.

Likewise, if you already have some savings earmarked for retirement, subtract what those savings will be worth when you retire from the result of Step 4. If necessary, you can use Table 5-1 from Step 3 to help you figure out how your current savings will grow over time.

Again, the table assumes inflation will run at 4% and your investment rate of return in retirement will be 6%. Also, the amounts in the table have been rounded to the most appropriate $100. Again, higher returns will reduce the amounts needed.

Table 5-3
Lump-Sum Value of Fixed Annual Payments

Annual Payment ➡ Lump-Sum Annual Value ➡	Anticipated Number of Years Will Spend in Retirement				
	15	20	25	30	35
$5,000	$64,600	$82,400	$98,400	$113,200	$126,400
$10,000	$129,200	$164,800	$196,800	$226,400	$252,800
$15,000	$193,800	$247,200	$295,200	$339,600	$379,200
$20,000	$258,400	$329,600	$393,600	$452,800	$505,600
$25,000	$323,000	$412,000	$492,000	$566,000	$632,000
$30,000	$387,600	$494,400	$590,400	$679,200	$758,400
$35,000	$452,200	$576,800	$688,800	$792,400	$884,800
$40,000	$516,800	$659,200	$787,200	$905,600	$1,011,200
$50,000	$646,000	$824,000	$984,000	$1,132,000	$1,264,000
$60,000	$775,200	$988,800	$1,180,800	$1,358,400	$1,516,800
$70,000	$904,400	$1,153,600	$1,377,600	$1,584,800	$1,769,600
$80,000	$1,033,600	$1,318,400	$1,574,400	$1,811,200	$2,022,400
$90,000	$1,162,800	$1,483,200	$1,771,200	$2,037,600	$2,275,200
$100,000	$1,292,000	$1,648,000	$1,986,000	$2,264,000	$2,528,000

Step 6. Compute personal monthly savings amount

After figuring the size of the leg of the stool for which you'll be responsible at retirement, it only remains to be determined how much you will need to set aside each month to reach that goal.

Another important assumption is necessary in order to do this: How much your investments will earn over time. If you assume your investment can earn 10%, you'll reach your goal faster than if you believe they'll only earn 6%. Choosing a rate of return largely is a function of your risk tolerance: the more risk you're willing to accept, the higher your potential return will be.

Once you've decided on an appropriate rate of return, Table 5-4 will quickly help you determine how much you need to set aside each month to accumulate the necessary nest egg you computed in Step 5. This table shows how much you will need to set aside each month for every $50,000 of nest egg you've figured you'll need. Thus, if in Step 4 your personal retirement savings needed to be $600,000, you would multiply the appropriate monthly payment from the table by 12 ($600,000/$50,000).

Several observations need to be made regarding this table. First, the figures were rounded to the next highest dollar. Next, these figures do not consider any income tax you would have to pay on your earnings. While taxes will lower your overall rate of return, people generally do not pay those taxes out of the funds they're saving for retirement. Finally, if you do some comparisons, you will quickly see how important it is to start saving for retirement early. It's always going to be easier to set aside $20 a month for 40 years than $289 a month for 10 years, regardless of your income level. Also, the second largest mistake I see people make, right behind not investing for retirement (in the first place), is being too conservative in the retirement investments. There is usually time to make up for any temporary losses.

Table 5-4
Monthly Savings Needed
per $50,000 of "Nest Egg"

Years Until Retirement	Assumed Rate of Return								
Monthly Saving	4%	5%	6%	7%	8%	9%	10%	11%	12%
40	$42	$33	$25	$19	$15	$11	$8	$6	$5
30	$73	$61	$50	$41	$34	$27	$23	$18	$15
20	$137	$122	$109	$96	$85	$75	$66	$58	$51
10	$340	$322	$306	$289	$274	$258	$245	$231	$218

Employer-Sponsored Retirement Plans

Retirement plans come in an amazing variety of shapes and sizes, however, they don't all work the same. Some promise to put in a certain amount (defined contribution), others to pay out a certain amount (defined benefit). Some allow you to defer part of your current salary, others are funded entirely by your employer. Some provide minimal tax incentives, others significant tax incentives, and still others only nominal tax incentives. The purpose of this section is to provide a general explanation of the many types of employer plans.

Employee Stock Ownership Plans (ESOP)

These are more or less profit sharing plans that are paid in the form of shares of the employer's stock instead of cash. If you participate in an ESOP, the value of your account rises and falls in conjunction with the change in the price of your employer's stock. One of the advantages of an ESOP is that it enables you to defer paying tax on any gain until you actually sell your shares.

Because ESOP's almost exclusively hold only employer's securities, there is little investment diversification in such plans. Therefore, employees over the age 55 who have been with a company more than 10 years must be allowed to diversify the assets in their ESOP accounts. Because of this lack of diversification, most employers offer ESOP in addition to some other form of retirement planning.

Simplified Employee Pension (SEP)

An SEP allows small businesses to avoid the intricate rules just described by, in essence, making annual contributions to their employee IRA's.

The maximum amount your employer can contribute to a SEP-IRA on your behalf is 15% of your salary (up to $22,500). This figure will change slightly each year.

If you are covered by a SEP, it is important for you to understand that once funds are placed in your SEP-IRA, they are your non-forfeitable property. They cannot be reclaimed at some later date by your employer. From that moment forward, the account is treated like any other IRA.

Contributory Plans

The tax law provides for a number of plans under which employees can defer part of their current income toward retirement, thus avoiding taxes on both the amounts deferred and on the earnings on those amounts until they are withdrawn from the plan.

Clearly, there are substantial benefits to be found in tax-favored retirement savings. Therefore, it is in your interest to be socking away into retirement savings the maximum amount your budget can possibly afford. Putting aside the maximum amount possible (or allowable under the law) can save you hundreds, even thousands of dollars off your annual tax bill. At the same time, you'll be helping yourself prepare for an increasingly uncertain future.

401(k) Plans

401(k) plans, named after the section of the tax law that created them, are the most common form of employer-sponsored contributory retirement plans. These plans usually allow you to designate a certain percentage of each paycheck to de deposited into an investment account (or accounts) on your behalf.

Your annual taxable salary is reduced by the amount you put into your 401(k). The tax law allows you to defer a maximum of $9,500 in income each year. The 1999 tax law allows you to defer a maximum of $10,000 in income each year. This figure is indexed for inflation every few years in $500 increments, and there is current legislation which, if passed, would increase this to $15,000. Your plan may have lower limits, and the maximum amount allowable is also subject to what is called "top-heavy rules."

Sometimes your employer will match all or part of the contributions you elect to defer. This means that, up to a certain percentage, for every dollar you contribute, your employer will fully or partially match your contribution. Over a period of time, through the vesting process described below, these matching contributions become your non-forfeitable property.

Matching funds increase the value of your contributions in two ways. First, it is a tax-deferred source of additional income. Your employer is giving you more money, but you don't pay tax on it until it's withdrawn. Second, the amounts your employer contributes grow on a tax-deferred basis. At an absolute minimum, then, you should contribute to your employer's 401(k) plan as much as your employer will match. If you don't, you're basically turning down "free" money.

Vesting is a process of transferring ownership of the employer contribution to the employee over a period of time. As an example, a vesting schedule might provide for a 20% ownership per year. On this basis, an employee would own all employer contributions after five years of participation or service with the employer. If an employee quit after the first year, they would only own, and be entitled to receive, 20% of the employer's contribution and the earnings on that money.

Tax-Sheltered Annuities (TSA or 403(b) Plans)

403(b) plan are available to employees of nonprofit organizations and public schools. You generally may contribute up to $9,500 per year. If you work for a health care, religious, or educational non-profit group, there also is a special provision in the law that lets you make so-called "catch-up" contributions to your 403(b) account, but only in $3,000 annual increments. This "catch-up" option probably won't be available to you if your regular contributions average more than $5,000 per year.

457 Plans

These plans are available to employees of state and local governments and nonprofit organizations. Under a 457 plan, you may defer as much as 25% of your salary, up to $7,500, to the plan each year.

The 457 plan also has a catch up provision. The catch up provision for the 457 provide that in each of the three years before your normal retirement age, you may contribute up to an additional $7,500 per year to your 457 plan, provided that you have deferred less than the maximum in earlier years.

One word of caution with regard to 457 plans: Unlike most of the other retirement plans we've discussed so far, the assets in a 457 plan are subject to the claims of your employer's creditors. In practical terms, this means that if your employer declares bankruptcy, the salary you've deferred might not be protected.

Salary Reduction Simplified Employer Pension (SARSEP)

SARSEP's are a simplified mechanism for your employer to make available to you the option of deferring income, if you work for a small business. As an employee, you still enjoy all of the advantages of deferring income, up to the same limits as with 401(k) plans. Similarly, as with 401(k) plans, your employer has the option of matching your contributions. In order to offer a SARSEP, the business must have fewer than 25 eligible employees. Not many small businesses have taken advantage of SARSEP's. Under the tax reform act of 1997, SARSEP's were replaced by the new simplified 401(k) plan.

Retirement Plans for the Self-Employed

Keoghs

Keogh plans essentially permit self-employed persons to establish and maintain defined benefit and defined contribution plans in much the same fashion as those discussed in the last section. The advantage to these plans is that they allow self-employed people to defer more of their income into retirement savings than is allowable with an IRA or SEP.

The higher contribution limits applicable to money purchase defined contribution plans and to defined benefit plans can be used when establishing a Keogh (with some technical adjustments).

The disadvantage is that they are more complex to administer and likely will require the assistance of a pension administration company.

SEP – Self Employed Pension

A self-employed SEP functions in much the same way as the employer SEP described in the last section, except that the maximum contribution percentage is lowered from 15% for employees to about 13.04% for the owner/employee. Once the funds are placed in a self-employed person's SEP-IRA, they are treated like any other IRA. In addition, as a self-employed person, you can establish a SARSEP for the benefit of your employees, but the total contribution for the year to your own account—SEP plus SARSEP—still cannot exceed 13.04% of your income.

One other advantage of an SEP is that contributions can be made anytime up to the date the owner's tax return is due, including extensions, assuming there is an existing account. This provides you with the flexibility to do some late tax planning, deciding as late as April (or August if you extend your return) how much you want to contribute to a SEP and deduct on your tax return.

In contrast, Keogh's allow deductions up until the due date of the return (without extensions), but only if the plan was in existence before the tax year in question ended. In short, Keogh provides more limited opportunities for after-the-fact tax planning than do SEP.

If you are a high-income self-employed person with a mature business, consider consulting with a pension plan administrator to see if a Keogh can be of benefit to you. If you are still a struggling entrepreneur, the SEP probably is a better bet right now.

Individual Retirement Accounts

Individual Retirement Accounts (IRA's) are a familiar part of the financial planning landscape. Before the 1986 overhaul of the tax laws, IRA's were a wonderful form of both tax-deductible and tax-advantaged savings. The deduction is much more limited now, but there are still benefits in IRA's.

IRA's are available in two ways, deductible and nondeductible. A deduction is based on whether or not you are covered by an employer's plan, and, if so, how much you make. Regardless of whether or not you can deduct your IRA contributions, they still can grow in the account on a tax-deferred basis. This feature may make even nondeductible IRA's an attractive investment.

The Tax Reform Act of 1997 (TRA97) considerably broadened the use of IRA's. Previous to TRA97, an individual who was not covered by an employer pension plan but who had a spouse that was covered, was usually ineligible to contribute to a deductible IRA. TRA97 liberalized this rule and opened the deductibility of the IRA to spouses of covered individuals as long as the combined income is $150,000 or less.

The most publicized addition to the IRA in the TRA97 is the Roth IRA. There are several important distinctions in the Roth that differ from the traditional IRA. Contributions into the Roth IRA, unlike the traditional IRA, are not deductible. The growth in the Roth IRA, however, continues to be tax-deferred. If you leave the funds in the Roth until 59½, you can withdraw the funds tax-free. This is a marked change from the traditional IRA which would be completely income taxable. There are also some situations where you can access the funds in your Roth prior to 59½, and still have no tax consequences. Generally, however, any withdrawal from the Roth prior to 59½ will be subject to ordinary income tax treatment and a 10% tax penalty.

Social Security Retirement Benefits

Social Security currently is the most important leg of the three-legged stool supporting many Americans in their retirement years. Monthly Social Security benefits mean the difference between poverty and relative comfort for a wide variety of recipients. For those of us in the planning stages, it is very important to understand the role Social Security benefits are likely to play in our retirement finances.

The Social Security Administration keeps track of the wages you receive. This is very important information, because it is used to compute your level of retirement benefits. It therefore is a good idea to double check their records—in fact, the agency encourages it. This can be done by submitting to the Social Security Administration (SSA) a form SSA-7004-sm. You can get this form by visiting your local Social Security office or calling 1-800-772-1213.

When you submit the form, the SSA will send you a Personal Earnings and Benefits Statement. This form often goes by its acronym, PEBES. Your PEBES will contain a complete printout of SSA's records regarding your annual earnings history. If there is a discrepancy between your records and the government's, the PEBES will tell you how to correct it.

Keep in mind you should check the SSA's records every three years. The SSA only guarantees to go back three years to correct any mistakes.

The Los Angeles Times has reported the administration will begin in the year 2000 to send to all social security participants benefit statements on an annual basis. The mailing costs alone are expected to be about $17 million per year

Withdrawals and Distributions of Retirement Savings

If you have been participating in some form of tax-deferred retirement plan—such as an IRA, SEP, 401(k), Keogh, or employer plan—you eventually will begin making withdrawals from your plan, voluntarily or involuntarily.

When it comes to your retirement savings, remember that if the funds in a retirement account were not taxed going in, they will be taxed coming out. Since most retirement savings occur on a pretax basis, this is an issue for most of us. Unfortunately, the stakes are higher than most people realize, and the margin of error is slim. If you make the wrong move, or through ignorance miss a tax-deferral opportunity, you could lose a hefty chunk of your retirement nest egg to unnecessary taxes. It therefore is important for you to learn the ways to minimize the tax bite on your retirement plan withdrawals and distributions.

In general, the longer you allow your retirement assets to enjoy the benefits of tax-deferred compounding, the better.

Strategies for Gays and Lesbians

Despite the AIDS epidemic, the truth is that most of us are going to live to see our so-called golden years. And, whether or not these years really turn out to be golden depends largely on how well we prepare for them.

The law gives a surviving spouse significant rights in a deceased spouse's non-contributory pension benefits. Unfortunately, none of those legal rights are available to domestic partners—or, for that matter, any other alternative family members. Lesbians and gay men usually can provide for their significant others in structuring pay-outs from an employer plan in retirement, but not in the case of premature death.

Many lesbians and gay men engage in moonlighting or freelancing work. This work is often an important supplement to a regular paycheck. Regardless of whether it pays for those little extras or is your main source of support, it's important to remember this income is eligible for a SEP contribution. Contributing 13.04% of your net income from moonlighting or freelancing will lower your tax bill this year, and allow the investment to grow without being taxed for many years, and help contribute to a more secure retirement. Although you have to fill out a very short form, you don't even have to file it with the IRS—just keep it in your permanent records.

Lesbians and gay couples cannot make espousal IRA contributions for their domestic partners. Prior to TRA97, the additional IRA contribution for someone with a non-working spouse was limited to $250. However, TRA97 increased that limit to $2,000 for the non-working spouse. This is a significant benefit not afforded to gays and lesbians.

Another major change regarding IRA's with TRA97 deals with the deductibility of one spouse's IRA when the other spouse has an employer-sponsored retirement plan. Prior to TRA97, one spouse could not deduct their IRA if the other spouse has a pension plan; the new law removed that condition.

Regarding Social Security benefits, they are one of the best deals going for married couples. Unfortunately, lesbians and gays are not eligible to claim such benefits. More importantly, they are not entitled to survival benefits if one of them dies. This means that lesbian and gay couples who are counting on Social Security retirement benefits to help meet their retirement income needs run the risk that a premature death—or even a death early in retirement—of a partner could severely affect and undermine their retirement planning. As with the lack of survivor rights for domestic partners in non-contributory employer plans, this risk may have to be managed through a combination of increased savings and life insurance.

Again, it often is advisable for gay couples to compute their retirement income needs individually, even if they save toward them jointly.

Chapter Six

Estate Planning
— The Basics

*Remember that money is of
a prolific generating nature.
Money can beget money, and its
offspring can beget more.*
—Ben Franklin

When a person dies (a *decedent*), a Byzantine set of rules kicks in to govern the distribution of the assets he or she owned at death (an *estate*). How these rules affect a particular decedent's estate depends on a number of variables: The size (i.e., value) of the estate, whether and which estate planning documents were in place when he or she died, and laws in the particular state or states having jurisdiction over the distribution of the decedent's estate. The important point here is that, although the word estate sounds like it only applies to rich people, if you own any assets when you die, you will leave behind an estate. Whether the distribution of the estate is smooth or bumpy— as well as whether it is expensive or economical—largely depends on how well you understand the process and plan for it.

There are two major areas of the law with which virtually all decedents' estates must contend: The state laws governing the distribution of a decedent's property (probate laws), and the federal and state laws taxing the transfer of a decedent's property (estate and inheritance taxes). While there's often a good bit of overlap between these two areas of the law, it's important to understand that they play separate roles in the estate planning process. It's also important to remember that what is included in your estate for purposes of one area of the law may not be included for the other.

A word of caution before we proceed: Estate planning is not a field for do-it-yourselfers. Of all the topics we've covered in this book, this is the most complicated one. Do not try going it on your own. Relying on the self-help books or software programs widely available at the local super store to create estate planning documents is a recipe for disaster. Admittedly, the estate planning process is expensive, probably more expensive for average folks than it needs to be. However, the only thing more expensive than engaging professional help is not engaging professional help. The rules are so numerous, and the mistakes are so irreversible, and their price is so high, that no mass-produced book or software program can give the level of assurance specific to your needs. For example, by the end of this chapter, you should be convinced that there's no such thing as a "simple" will and no way to cut corners in estate planning. So, let's be blunt: Estate planning is for professionals.

What's in your estate?

When you die, your estate is made up of all the property you leave behind. To give you a sense of how broad this definition is, consider the following list of assets included in your estate:

- All the real estate you own.

- Houses, boats, and other vehicles.

- The entire contents of your house(s), including clothing, jewelry, furniture, rugs, china, crystal, silver, artwork, electronics, and so on.

- Bank accounts.

- Stocks, bonds, mutual funds, and other investments.

- The value of life insurance policies you own (if you are the person insured, then the full death benefit).

- Annuities.

- Retirement accounts and pension plan balances.

- Money owed to you at the time of your death, from unpaid interest and dividends to income tax refunds and legal claims arising from the cause of your death.

- Debts you owe that are forgiven when you die.

- Gifts you've given within three years of your death, but only if they were made with certain "strings" attached (for example, you retained some interest in the gift or some right to control what happened to the gift).

- The death benefit from any policies insuring your life that someone else owns, if you used to own them and transferred them within three years of your death.

- Any type of business interest you owned.

- All assets of the business if it's a sole proprietorship.

- Your proportional share of the business if it's a partnership.

- Your shares of stock if it's a corporation or limited liability company.

Distributions of Property and the Probate Process

When you die, the assets you leave behind legally pass to others in one of four ways:

1. Automatically ("by operation of law" in legalese) because you owned a particular asset jointly with another person and the title to the property included a right of survivorship, as with a house or a bank account.

2. Through the designation of another person as a beneficiary in the documents governing the ownership of the asset, as with a beneficiary designation of a life insurance policy or a retirement account.

3. Through the provisions of a valid trust.

4. Through the probate laws of the state having jurisdiction over your property. If property doesn't pass as a result of survivorship, beneficiary designation, or trust, it has to pass through probate. Probate can be a long, costly and unnecessary procedure.

Unified Credit

The *Unified Credit* is the primary way that the tax law attempts to protect small to average-size estates from the bite of the federal estate tax. The first $650,000 of your taxable estate usually is not subject to the federal estate tax. This $650,000 is one of the most important figures in estate tax planning. The TRA97 has increased the Unified Credit from $600,000 up to $1-million over the next several years. For 1999, the Unified Credit amount is $650,000, which translates to a tax credit of $207,000. When the Unified Credit reaches $1-million in 2006, it will remain fixed.

Wills and Will Substitutes

A *will* is a document that provides for the legal transfer of your assets after you die, names a person to settle your estate, and names a guardian for your minor children. Wills are fundamental estate-planning documents, and it is highly unlikely that you will emerge from the planning process without one.

Things You Can't Do in a Will

There are a surprisingly small number of things the probate law will not permit you to do in your will. For example, there are a very few people you simply cannot disinherit through a will. All states have laws to prevent you from disinheriting a spouse, and some states also make it difficult to disinherit children; usually you cannot do so if they're minors. Also, you can't ask your beneficiaries to do something that's illegal or against "public policy" in order to receive their bequest (for example, get married or join a certain club). In some states, it's either difficult or not possible to persuade a court to enforce an *in terrorem* clause in your will (i.e., a clause that says challengers to the will get nothing). In other states, it's not a problem to do so.

The biggest problem with a will for gays and lesbians is that all wills are subject to probate. Probate is derived from the Latin word *provo*, which means "to prove." The probate process is designed for beneficiaries to prove their claim against an estate; thus they are subject to challenge in a court of law. This means a family can actually change the entire intent of your will, and your partner can lose all the rights you had intended for him or her. It is not uncommon for a gay lover to be thrown out of their home by a family member who challenged a will in court.

Trusts

Trusts have a long and distinguished history in assisting people in transferring and managing their property. Flexibility and a largely self-directed nature make trusts an important tool in the financial and estate-planning arsenal.

There are three main players in any trust:

The *settler* (also referred to as the *grantor* or the *donor*; the three terms usually can be used interchangeably) is the person who places assets into the trust.

The *trustee* is the person or institution that agrees to hold the assets and administer them in accordance with the terms of the trust.

The *beneficiary* (or beneficiaries) is the person (or persons) entitled to receive some benefit from the trust — either income generated by the assets the trust holds, or distributions of those assets under conditions specified in the trust document, or both. These beneficiaries, called an *income beneficiary* and a *residuary beneficiary,* respectively, need not be the same person.

Trusts can become operative at one of two points in time.

Living trusts (also known as *inter vivos trusts*) are established while you are alive. Assets are transferred into the trust at the time it is created, and the trust operates during your lifetime.

Testamentary trusts are created in your will (as in "last will and testament"), are funded by bequests made in your will, and only operate after your death. They are administered by a trustee you name in your will. Note this trustee need not be the same person as the personal representative named in your will to administer your estate.

Pour-over trusts are created while you're alive but funded when you die. They often are used to receive and distribute life insurance proceeds, retirement benefits, or residuary bequests from your will.

The other important characteristic for any trust is whether or not it is permanent. In legalese, trusts are said to be either *revocable* or *irrevocable.*

In a **revocable trust**, the settler reserves the right to amend or revoke the trust, change the conditions under which the assets are held, or reclaim the assets for his or her own use. Because assets in a revocable trust are distributed in accordance with the terms of the trust, they are not subject to the jurisdiction of the probate court when you die. This makes revocable trusts an important estate planning tool for people whose goal is to avoid probate.

In an **irrevocable trust**, the settler relinquishes all rights to the assets in the trust. He or she cannot later have a change of heart and try to alter the terms of the trust or reclaim some or all of the assets for his or her own use. Because the transfer is irrevocable, assets placed into these trusts not only avoid the jurisdiction of the probate court, but they usually are removed from your gross estate. This makes irrevocable trusts valuable tools for estate tax planning.

One other thing of which you should be aware with regard to trusts is that they may be separate taxpaying entities. The general rule of thumb here is that revocable trusts are not separate tax-paying entities; the income they earn is taxed to the settler of the trust. Irrevocable trusts usually are separate taxpaying entities, and the trustee must file an income tax return for the trust and pay any tax due out of the trust's assets.

There are some important exceptions to this general rule (i.e., sometimes revocable trusts are separate taxpaying entities), so be sure to ask your estate planner who pays the taxes on your trust's income.

Another aspect of trusts and income taxes is that when Congress tinkered with the tax law in 1993, it severely compressed the bracket structure used to compute trusts' taxes. Trusts now find themselves in the top income tax bracket—39.6%—when their income exceeds $7,900. A single person, in contrast, doesn't reach this rate until his or her income is over $263,750 (these 1996 figures are adjusted annually for inflation).

Trusts always had more compact rate structures than people, and this isn't necessarily wrong in theory, but the 1993 change was downright harsh and has made planning very difficult. If your trust is going to have to pay taxes, this is another issue you should explore in depth with your planner.

Revocable Living Trusts as Will Substitutes

One of the most common uses of the revocable living trust is as a probate avoidance device. What you do is create a revocable living trust, name yourself and a friend, loved one, or trusted advisor as co-trustees, and transfer all of the assets you own into it. The trust specifies that all of the income is to be paid to you for your life, and further specifies what is to be done with all of the trust assets when you die.

Other Common Uses of Trusts

In addition to probate minimization, there are several other important uses of trusts in the estate-planning process:

1. **Minimizing estate taxes.** Certain testamentary trusts are an important tool used by married couples to minimize their estate taxes. Under a *Credit Shelter* trust, the first spouse to die leaves part of his estate in a trust for the couple's heirs, thereby ensuring that the trust's assets are not included in the gross estate of the surviving spouse when she dies. In a QTIP trust, a surviving spouse receives only a special right to lifetime income and support from the trust's assets, thereby also avoiding the inclusion of those assets in his or her gross estate.

2. **Holding property for minors.** Since minors are not permitted to own property in their own names, trusts can be an excellent way to hold and manage property for them. Such trusts generally are testamentary, having been created under a family member's will, but they can be inter vivos as well. In most states, trusts are not subject to the same restrictions as custodial accounts. One key difference between trusts for minors and custodial accounts is that minors can claim the assets in a custodial account once they reach the age of majority, whereas the settler decides at what age they get the

assets in a trust. On the flip side, trusts entail both set-up and ongoing administration expenses. The tax burden on a trust may be higher or lower than the tax burden on a custodial account, depending on how the tax rules apply to children under age 14 (kiddie tax rules).

3. **Protecting beneficiaries.** If you are concerned that one or more of your beneficiaries may not be responsible with the assets you want to give them, consider placing those assets in a trust with a spendthrift clause. Such a clause prohibits a beneficiary from borrowing against the trust's assets or future income, and protects the trust from the beneficiary's creditors. Of course, once money goes out of the trust and to the beneficiary, creditors have complete access to it. However, since spendthrift provisions usually give the trustee discretion to determine whether, when, how much, or to whom to pay a beneficiary's share of the trust's income, they are very effective in protecting irresponsible people from themselves.

4. **Holding a life insurance policy.** Irrevocable trusts can be established to hold a life insurance policy, the proceeds from which are intended to be used to pay the estate taxes of the person insured by the policy. By having the trust own the policy, the amount of the death benefit is not included in the gross estate of the insured when he or she dies. (Remember, the owner of a policy and the insured don't have to be the same person.) These trusts, therefore, are very popular estate tax planning vehicles for high-net-worth individuals who are certain to owe estate taxes.

5. **Qualifying for Medicaid.** In order to insure that the costs of long-term nursing care services do not deplete a person's estate, a Medicaid qualifying trust can be

established. It will hold those assets which would otherwise create a net worth too high to qualify for Medicaid. There are several important requirements in order to successfully implement this controversial strategy, so consult an attorney who specializes in this area of law.

Gifts

In general, the tax law allows each person to give away up to $10,000 dollars (cash or property) per recipient per year free of federal gift tax. This amount is called the *annual exclusion*. It's important to remember that you have an unlimited number of annual exclusions—but they're only worth $10,000 each. Another way of saying this is, you can give gifts to an unlimited number of different people, but you can't give more than $10,000 worth of cash or property to any one person each year without having to worry about federal gift taxes.

For a straight married couple, each spouse each can give away $10,000 to any one person, for a total of $20,000 a year free of federal tax. In 1998, the $10,000 annual exclusion was indexed for inflation in $1,000 increments.

None of the federal gift tax rules applies to gifts made to a recognized charity. There are no limits on the amount you can contribute to one or more charities, and those gifts are never subject to the federal gift tax. There are limits on the amount of charitable contributions you can claim as an itemized deduction for income tax purposes, but that's a different matter.

The law places the burden of paying any gift tax on the person who made the gift. However, if the IRS can't collect from the donor, there are provisions in the law enabling them to go after the person who received the gift for the tax due.

Estate Tax Planning Techniques

If your gross estate—or your combined gross estates if you are married—exceeds $650,000 in 1999, or if it is likely to reach that threshold before you die, you probably need to be concerned about the federal estate tax. Take a moment now to review the list of what's included in your gross estate, and try to think of something not on this list. You'll quickly get a sense of how all-encompassing the federal estate tax is.

When you add these inventoried assets together, it is not hard to see that more people than expected have to worry about the federal estate tax. A house that's paid off, some life insurance, a solid pension plan, a little nest egg in the bank, and that magical $650,000 figure can quickly start closing in!

One technique for minimizing estate taxes involves annual gifting. When you give money or other property away, it's obviously no longer yours. The $10,000 gift tax annual exclusion is often an ideal solution to potential estate tax problems for people whose net worth is right on the border of the $650,000 threshold.

Another essential estate-planning tool, available only to married couples, is known as the *marital deduction.* The marital deduction is unlimited, which means that you can give as much as you want to your spouse, while you're living or when you die, and not pay gift or estate tax on it.

For certain high-net-worth people, it is an option that must be given serious consideration. This benefit given to spouses is not available to gay and lesbian couples. Beyond the obvious altruistic and societal benefits of charitable giving, certain provisions of the tax law make such gift a financially attractive option.

First, any amounts you leave to a qualified charity are deducted from your gross estate for federal estate tax purposes. Thus, outright charitable gifts made in a will sometimes can solve all of one's estate tax problems. However, any assets given to a charity outright will be unavailable to pass on to a spouse or partner. There are some techniques you can use through charitable trusts which would benefit your beneficiary as well as the charity. These are known as Charitable Remainder or Charitable Lead trusts.

Strategies and Issues for Gays and Lesbians

Of all the aspects of financial planning, nowhere are our issues more profound than in the area of estate planning. Whether single or part of a couple, gay people face an enormous set of challenges in planning their affairs around an insensitive to downright homophobic probate system and a generally unfriendly tax regime.

A challenge to one's will by hostile family members is a major concern for many people in our community, particularly for those of us who want to provide for our alternative families.

If the potential of your will being challenged is a serious concern for you, there are steps you can take to minimize the risk.

First, fully explore all the will alternatives discussed above—beneficiary designations, joint ownership, and trusts. A will challenge only threatens the assets in your probate estate, so if there's not much there, there's not much risk. Next, be certain your will mentions each and every member of your family, even if it's to politely disinherit them. Third, if you face AIDS or some other life-threatening illness, be certain to execute your will early. Finally, if you are leaving the bulk of your estate to a significant other, be certain that he or she is not in the room when you execute the will, that your witnesses take note of his or her absence, and that you tell them you are under no duress or undue influence from him or her to execute the will. If your witnesses believe you were of sound mind and not under undue influence, it will be very hard for someone else to convince a judge otherwise. It is also recommended that you update your trust every few years. This will help to prove your intent in creating the trust during a challenge.

The federal gift tax rules threaten to create some serious burdens for lesbian and gay couples. In theory, here's the issue: If living expenses aren't split equally, it's quite likely that one partner is making a gift to another. If you think this is a concern for you and your other half, there are things you can do to ensure that you're treated fairly. First, be scrupulous about the paper trail. Make sure that you can document what each of you contributed to joint expenditures, so there's no possibility of the IRS arguing that a gift was made when there was none.

Naming fiduciaries can be a risky proposition for lesbians and gay men who expect their estate planning wishes to be questioned by family members. Even if you think your family is supportive, that premise is nowhere put to the test quite like it is when you die. The stakes are even higher for a gay couple, who presumably would be inclined to name each other as their fiduciaries.

Chapter Seven

The Need for
Collateral Documents

*To get profit without risk, experience without danger, and reward
without work, is as impossible as it is to live without being born.*
—Gouthey

In addition to traditional estate planning documents, the uncertain
legal status of lesbians, gay men, and their relationships forces many
of us to consider the need for a number of so-called collateral planning documents. Our ability to ensure that our preferences and relationships are respected in the event of our illness or death is increased
by many of these documents: Powers of attorney for financial matters, health care powers of attorney, advance medical directives, living
wills, and directives regarding the disposition of our remains when we
die. For some of us, circumstances also dictate a need to plan for the
contingency that a relationship will end. Domestic partnership agreements are as much a reality for our community as prenuptial agreements are for the dominant culture.

While our community tends to perceive many of these planning issues as significant, a partner's hostile relatives may shut out
the decision-making process in times of crisis. It is important to

remember that gay people have built families of many kinds. Even if you are not part of a "couple," it is possible there are people in your life you trust more than your family to make important decisions in times of crisis. The law will not honor your priorities unless you articulate them clearly and properly in advance.

It also is important to remember that the documents we are going to discuss are largely creatures of state law. Whether these documents are available in your state, and the extent to which they will be respected by a potentially homophobic legal system, vary widely. It is critical that you seek competent and well-informed legal advice when you do planning in this area.

Granting Powers

A *power of attorney* is a document that authorizes another person to act on your behalf. There is a unique syntax to the world of powers of attorney, so some initial definitions are in order. The person granting the power of attorney to another is called the *principal*. The person receiving the power is called the *attorney-in-fact* (some people refer to this person as the *agent,* but attorney-in-fact is more precise). Although the document is known as a power of attorney, we'll refer to it as the *power* or the *powers* for short.

Powers can be as broad or narrow as the principal desires. They can take effect immediately upon execution of the document, or they can be triggered by the principal's incapacity or incompetence. How broad the powers should be, and when they should be effective, depend on what they're to be used for and to whom you're granting them.

General Power of Attorney

A *general power of attorney* gives another person the authority to transact business on your behalf. It usually gives your attorney-in-fact access to your bank and brokerage accounts, the authority to sell property on your behalf, the authority to deal with insurance companies, and generally the authority to handle any other aspect of your financial affairs on your behalf.

116

The process for drafting powers is becoming increasingly technical and sophisticated, so lawyers now frequently include detailed lists of the powers a principal is granting. A principal gives an attorney-in-fact extraordinary powers, so it is critical that you choose your attorney-in-fact carefully.

You can limit a power to a specific asset or group of assets, exclude a particular asset or group of assets from a broad delegation of powers, or even execute a power limited to one specific transaction.

Unless your document specifies otherwise, a power of attorney is effective upon execution. Historically, powers were used to enable principals to have business transacted at a distance. An attorney-in-fact could act on behalf of a faraway principal, or could serve in the event of a principal's extended absence. While modern transportation and communications largely have vitiated this use of the power of attorney, the properly drafted power remains a very effective way to ensure that your finances are handled in the event of your illness, incapacity, or disability.

All states now permit powers to survive a principal's incapacity, provided that the document specifically states that the principal intends this result. This is called a *durable power of attorney*, and it is the form that most powers take when drafted as a tool for incapacity planning.

Powers of attorney are governed by state law, and what the law requires in order for a power to be valid varies widely from state to state. It is important that your power of attorney be executed in compliance with your state's legal requirements. These execution formalities usually cover witness or notarization requirements, but it is important that you comply with all requirements regardless of the form they take. Also, if you routinely reside in more than one state, ideally you should execute separate powers in and for each state. At a realistic minimum, however, make sure your power of attorney satisfies the execution formalities of the stricter state.

Advance Directives (Living Wills) and Health Care Powers

Financial matters aren't the only concerns a person can have in the event of incapacity. Interacting with the health care behemoth becomes a major concern for those within its grasp. Decisions regarding medical treatment, termination of medical treatment, and the use of life-sustaining measures need to be made routinely in a health care emergency. In the event you are unable to make these decisions, it is critical that you express your preferences clearly and correctly while you are healthy, and that, if you wish to designate someone else to make medical decisions for you, you do so in advance. In the absence of such documents, it is a patient's next of kin or the system itself that will make all health care decisions. For gays and lesbians, the next of kin may be the last person we want making that decision.

Health Care Powers of Attorney

A *durable power of attorney* for health care matters functions in the medical realm in about the same way general powers of attorney function in the financial realm. A principal grants powers to an attorney-in-fact to make health care decisions in the event the principal is unable to do so for one's self.

The rules regarding durability, execution, and revocation of health care powers usually are identical to those for financial powers. The powers granted to an attorney-in-fact for health care decisions can be broad or limited, although it is almost always advisable to grant the broadest possible powers. Health care providers are understandably litigation-shy, and the more assurances you can give them in your document, the better.

Advance Medical Directives (Living Wills)

Many people have a basic understanding of advance medical directives, more generally known as *living wills*, as documents that tell doctors and hospitals not to prolong their lives by using artificial means in the event they become terminally or incurably ill or injured, or lapse into what the medical profession sometimes refers to as a "chronic vegetative state." When you can't speak for yourself, the living will tells the health care system what treatments you do not consent to.

A key aspect of a good living will is a clear statement of what procedures you want withheld and under what circumstances. Within the confines of your state's laws, your living will should spell out specifically which procedures you wish withheld in the event you are terminally ill and incapable of granting or withholding consent. These include such procedures as artificial respiration or ventilation, heart pumps, dialysis, the administration of food and water, and the administration of pain-killing medications. In many states, if you fail to specify your preferences, there is a "default" preference the health care provider will be required to follow. This default may be at odds with your personal wishes, so it is best to be as specific as possible.

It is important to understand that there are no ironclad guarantees that a living will is going to be honored in all situations. In some states, living wills are only "advisory" or a "guide" for your health care providers. The best way to minimize the possibility of unfortunate outcomes is to execute both a living will and a health care power. That way, if the medical establishment cannot or will not honor your wishes, your power-of-attorney can use his or her authority to either litigate the issue or change your health care providers. In some states, the durable health care power of attorney is the "stronger" of the two documents. Thus, the combination of a living will and a health care power is about as close as one gets to a guarantee in these matters.

Living Wills

In the absence of a valid living will, the health care establishment sometimes sees fit to ignore the decisions of even biological next of kin in these matters. It therefore is critical that any person who does not wish to receive extraordinary life-sustaining measures properly executes the necessary paperwork.

Priority of Visitation

There's one other aspect of interacting with the health care system that is of critical importance to gay people, and unique to our circumstances. When one is in a hospital or other in-patient facility, it traditionally is one's biological next of kin who decides who gets to visit and when (within medical limits, of course). Lesbians and gay men can find themselves cut off from their life partners in devastating ways by family members who have barred them from hospital rooms and so on.

Although there can be no ironclad guarantee that it will be honored, it is critical that your health care powers grant to your attorney-in-fact what's known as a *priority of visitation*. A priority of visitation basically says that your attorney-in-fact gets to see you before anyone else, including biological family members. It usually also gives your attorney-in-fact the power to decide who else can—and cannot—visit you. It's important that the wording of this power be brutally direct. Language such as "in preference over my blood relatives" is not out of line.

Directives Regarding Disposition of Remains

In all states, decisions regarding a decedent's final arrangements are made by the person's next of kin. At the same time, although durable powers of attorney survive a person's incapacity, they do not survive his or her death. To put it more bluntly, they expire when the principal does. Accordingly, a power of attorney cannot be used to direct the disposition of a principal's remains.

In some states, a person can execute a document directing the disposition of their remains or authorizing another person to make those arrangements for them. Usually, final arrangements are also discussed (and paid for) through a person's will and/or living trust.

Domestic Partnership Agreements

When a couple gets married, the state hands them a domestic partnership agreement in the form of the various laws governing the sharing of assets, income, and expenses. For an unmarried couple, however, there are few, if any, laws governing the sharing of assets, income, and expenses. Such a couple needs a domestic partnership agreement in order to set adequate ground rules for such matters.

Whether or not to enter into a domestic partnership agreement is probably one of the most difficult choices a lesbian or gay couple must make. This is not to suggest that the decision to actually form the domestic partnership will be difficult. It's just that writing down how it should end can prove delicate, to say the least. A domestic partnership agreement is like admitting in advance that the relationship isn't going to work.

It may be helpful to keep a little perspective here. In some sense, the decision regarding the domestic partnership agreement is not all together unlike the prenuptial agreements many heterosexuals enter into shortly before the "I do's." If these agreements make sense for people who receive all the legal trimmings that come with marriage, doesn't it seem reasonable to assume that we need them at least as much?

Strategies for Gays and Lesbians

A crisis can cause the best, most supportive family members to behave irrationally. The law will not respect our relationships unless we force it to. Combined with the other documents and techniques discussed in this book, the durable power of attorney for financial matters is designed to ensure that respect.

Single lesbians and gay men often share the same need for an attorney-in-fact as their "coupled" counterparts. The specter of illness is, of course, a very real issue for many in our community. Beyond that, however, lies the real risk for many of us that, if we suddenly found ourselves incapacitated, our financial decisions might not be made in accordance with our wishes or by people who respect our priorities. It is quite likely that, absent a power of attorney, family members who may or may not be supportive of our lifestyles and sensitive to our needs will be called on to handle our finances in the event of an emergency. All lesbians and gay men should consider carefully the need for a power of attorney. While it is essential for those of us with significant others, it likely is equally critical for many of the rest of us. Appointing a trusted friend or business adviser as our attorney-in-fact may better serve our needs than relying on the judgment of family member.

With regard to health care, lesbian and gay people need to prepare for three particular contingencies:

1. Providing instructions regarding life-sustaining procedures.

2. Designating who will make health care decisions for us in the event of our incapacity.

3. Ensuring that those individuals important to us have access to us while we a incapacitated.

The previously mentioned documents will go a long way in helping you achieve your desired planning results. Putting into action the financial advice in this book and creating these documents can create the level of security and prosperity you desire. I thank you for taking the initiative to complete this book and I wish you the best. If you have not already done so, my advice at this point is to take action !

One of the most important things you can do to help achieve your financial goals is to come out of the closet. Until you come out, you cannot ask your employer for domestic partner benefits, you cannot ask your state legislature to provide the infrastructure that comes with legal sanction for your relationship, you cannot attack homophobic practices in the insurance industry, you cannot ask a bank or a hospital to honor your partner's power of attorney, and you cannot explain your estate plan to your family. These are just a few of the broad range of financial planning objectives that you'll have trouble achieving until you're out. However, most important of all, you cannot fully achieve the desired peace of mind that brought you to the financial planning process in general and this book in particular until you never again are forced to hide who you are. When it comes to a solid financial plan, coming out is essential to the process.

—Todd Rainey

To Reach Todd Rainey

Mail: Rainey, Kiley and Associates
15456 Ventura Blvd. #202
Sherman Oaks, CA 91403
Phone: (888) 393-3300 (Toll free)
or; Phone: (818) 788-4719
Fax: (818) 788-5943

e-mail: TRainey963@aol.com

Order Form
for additional products to support your financial and emotional growth

1. ***Wealth On Any Income***, by Rennie Gabriel, CLU, CFP. $17.95
This **book** is designed to assist people in creating work as a choice, instead of a requirement. It covers the emotional and practical keys to handling money effectively. People will learn how to:

- Be rich on any income. Live within your income in 90 days, guaranteed!
- Get out of credit card debt, easily and forever.
- Handle emergency spending without creating a financial disaster.
- Save 10–20% of income, and have it in the bank or investments.
- Set and achieve financial, career, or any goals, and have others support you.

2. ***Wealth On Any Income.*** This two hour **cassette tape and workbook program** presented by the author guides people through the process of establishing their financial goals, setting up a spending plan (instead of budget), structuring credit card debt to eliminate it, creating a technique to know how much money you have for any category of expenses in less than 10 seconds, **without a computer,** and much, much more. Program investment: $59.00

3. ***Couples and Money***, *A Couples' Guide for the New Millennium*, by Victoria F. Collins. Money affects a relationship as much as love, and arguing over money is the leading cause of divorce. This **book** is a vital guide on how couples can thrive financially and emotionally by providing instructions and exercises on safe conversations around money. It covers everything from buying groceries to easing the pressure of a two-career marriage. Recommended by Consumer Credit Counseling Service. Over 20,000 copies sold. $13.95

******

To order any of the products listed above, e-mail to renniecoach@earthlink.net or you may **CALL** (800) 940-2622 and use a MasterCard or Visa, or **FAX** the form on the following page to (818) 990-8631, or **MAIL** to:

The Financial Coach, Inc.
14340 Addison St. #101,
Sherman Oaks, CA 91423

Order Form

Name _____

Address _____ Daytime Phone (   )_____

City _____State _____ Zip Code _____

Product Description	Quantity	
_____	_____	$_____
_____	_____	$_____
_____	_____	$_____
	Sub total $	_____
(Only for orders delivered in CA) Sales Tax 8.25% +		_____
Shipping & handling, $5 per book or tape +		_____
	Total $	_____

❑ Check enclosed (payable to The Financial Coach, Inc.)

❑ Please charge my M/C or Visa #_____

Signature as on the credit card_____

Expiration Date_____

To learn how you can become a published author contact:

The Financial Coach, Inc.
14340 Addison St. #101
Sherman Oaks, CA 91423
(800) 940-2622 Fax (818) 990-8631
e-mail: renniecoach@earthlink.net
www.InstantAuthor.com